The Independent Homesteader

A Handbook for Off-Grid Living Success

Jordan Johson

Table of Contents

INTRODUCTION

Thank you for visiting "The Independent Homesteader: A Handbook for Off-Grid Living Success." In the following pages, you'll embark on a journey towards self-sufficiency, gaining the knowledge and tools that empower individuals to thrive off the grid. This manual is more than just a guide- it's a blueprint for those who aspire to be self-reliant, environmentally conscious, and deeply connected to the land.

Homesteading has a long history based on resiliency, ingenuity, and a close relationship with the natural world. "The Independent Homesteader" is designed for contemporary pioneers—people prepared to take on the rigors and benefits of life off the grid. Regardless of your driving force—a desire to withdraw from the city, take up environmental stewardship, or lead a more sustainable lifestyle—this book offers the helpful advice you need to tran

As we explore the upcoming chapters, you will learn the essential components of living off the grid. Each chapter thoroughly examines important subjects, from determining your level of readiness and choosing the best site to constructing your homestead and incorporating sustainable practices. Discover the secrets of sustainable agriculture, off-grid energy alternatives, and water management. You'll also discover how to preserve your harvests and lead a more independent existence.

"The Independent Homesteader" focuses on thriving rather than just getting by. Explore chapters on creating a supportive community, incorporating technology into your farm, and being self-sufficient daily. Discover the money management techniques that enable self-sufficient living and read about the achievements of prosperous homesteaders who have gone before you.

Thus, let this manual be your companion whether you're an experienced homesteader seeking fresh perspectives or a beginner envisioning a life off the grid. Let's journey together to achieve autonomous homesteading and a more contented, environmentally friendly lifestyle.

CHAPTER I

Assessing Readiness

Mental Preparedness

One of the most critical aspects of practical off-grid living is mental readiness, which is frequently overlooked even though it can substantially impact an individual's capacity to survive in a lifestyle associated with self-sufficiency. A solid mental fortitude and the ability to adapt are required to progress toward independence. This is in addition to the necessary physical skills and practical knowledge. When it comes to homesteading, the difficulties can be as varied as the answers, and having a mindset ready to face them is the most critical factor differentiating those who only survive from those who actually thrive.

Off-grid living requires a profound knowledge of the necessary commitment, which is one of the critical components of mental readiness related to this lifestyle. The decision to live a homesteading lifestyle is not fleeting; instead, it is a profound and long-lasting commitment to a way of life that requires resiliency in the face of challenges. The mental preparation needed to negotiate the hurdles of isolation, fluctuating weather conditions, and the demands of feeding oneself and one's family through self-sufficiency is comparable to preparing oneself for a voyage that will last a lifetime. The homesteader must cultivate an unyielding desire to meet challenges head-on and develop inventive solutions. This requires the homesteader to forego the advantages of contemporary urban living in favor of a more profound relationship with nature.

Cultivating a positive attitude toward the uncertainties inherent in off-grid living is another component of mental readiness. Self-sufficient individuals must acquire the ability to accept and adjust to the unpredictability of nature to establish themselves as independent. The mental fortitude of a homesteader is put to the test regularly, whether it be in the form of dealing with unforeseen weather patterns, difficulties with crops, or breakdowns in equipment. Those who approach these obstacles with a mindset focused on problem-solving, learning, and growth are better suited to withstand the storms, both literally and figuratively, that come with living off the grid.

Regarding mental readiness, another essential component is the capacity to adjust to new circumstances. Off-grid life frequently necessitates making adjustments to one's goals and expectations regularly. Homesteaders need to be psychologically flexible and able to reevaluate and adjust their objectives and plans in response to various challenges, including changes in the weather and unanticipated obstacles in the building or agricultural industries. Ensuring that setbacks do not become insurmountable obstacles but rather opportunities for creative problem-solving and personal development is essential to mental preparedness. This may be accomplished by cultivating an adaptable mindset that can change when specific circumstances require it.

To add insult to injury, homesteading presents unique social and psychological obstacles. Finding strategies to deal with and even flourish in solitude is essential to mental preparation because the isolation that frequently comes with an off-grid living may be mentally exhausting. One's mental health must cultivate a strong feeling of community, even if it is done remotely, through the sharing of experiences, the establishment of online networks, and the holding of occasional get-togethers. The ability to discover joy and purpose inside oneself and within the homesteading lifestyle, without external validation, is a sign of mental readiness that supports persons through the inevitable periods of solitude they will experience.

As an additional point of interest, mental readiness in off-grid life incorporates a comprehensive approach to overall health and wellness. There is a direct connection between a homesteader's mental resilience and their total health, in addition to the fact that physical and mental health are deeply related. In addition to being lifestyle choices, getting enough sleep, maintaining a healthy diet, and engaging in regular physical activity are all critical components of mental readiness. Because homesteading is such a strenuous activity, people must be in the best possible psychological and physical shape to meet the obstacles that arise daily with motivation and concentration.

In conclusion, those who embrace the independent homesteading lifestyle must emphasize the importance of mental preparedness as a critical factor in their success. This is not merely a mental state; it is a dynamic quality that develops and becomes more pronounced over time. By cultivating resilience, adaptability, and a positive mindset, the homesteader committed to their endeavors ensures that mental fortitude becomes a driving force behind their road toward self-sufficiency. When the difficulties of living off the grid become more apparent, those individuals who have made an effort to mentally prepare themselves find that they cannot only survive but also thrive in the lifestyle of an independent homesteader, which is immensely satisfying and sustainable.

Financial Considerations

To determine whether or not a self-sufficient lifestyle is feasible and whether or not it can be maintained over time, financial concerns play a critical role in the success of off-grid living. Homesteading, which strongly focuses on self-sufficiency and resiliency, necessitates a sophisticated approach to financial matters that deviates from the standards typically associated with urban living. Regarding finances, living off the grid requires careful planning, various ways of generating revenue, and shifting toward alternative economic systems such as bartering and trading. In negotiating these factors, persons beginning the journey of independent homesteading learn the delicate balance between being financially self-sufficient and being resourceful in adapting to the unpredictability of nature and rural living.

Off-grid life requires a realistic assessment of one's resources and a disciplined approach to budgeting to be financially prepared. This is the cornerstone of financial preparedness. Homesteaders may suffer swings in their income, seasonal differences in production, and unanticipated expenses. This contrasts urban living, which typically makes it easier to implement regular financial planning due to a consistent wage. It is necessary to have a detailed budget that considers both fixed and variable costs. It is essential to have a comprehensive awareness of the resources needed for the homestead to be maintained. These resources include the production of food, the management of water, the energy systems, and the upkeep of infrastructure.

In addition, planning finances for off-grid living goes beyond the current need and encompasses the long-term sustainability of the lifestyle. To lower their long-term expenses, homesteaders should think about making investments in infrastructure that is both long-lasting and energy-efficient. Among these are the initial expenses associated with installing renewable energy systems, effective water-harvesting technologies, and durable building materials. The initial investments may appear large; nonetheless, they contribute to the homestead's ability to become financially self-sufficient by reducing the amount of money spent on recurring expenses and increasing the homestead's capacity to withstand the test of time.

Diversification of revenue sources is another essential component of independent homesteading that must be taken into consideration from a financial standpoint. It might be risky to rely only on a single source of income, particularly in circumstances where the influence of external economic forces may be limited. Homesteaders frequently investigate a variety of ways to generate revenue, including the sale of surplus vegetables, handmade crafts, or livestock. Furthermore, adopting the sharing economy, which involves sharing access to goods and services rather than owning them, by renting out spare space or equipment can be a significant contributor to achieving financial security. For example, if you have an unused barn, you could rent it for events or storage. The ability to adapt to new circumstances and make use of a wide range of abilities in order to generate income is a defining characteristic of financial preparation in off-grid living.

Off-grid life gives renewed importance to the traditional economic activities of bartering and trading, which extend back to a time before contemporary monetary systems were developed. Within this discussion, financial issues go beyond the traditional transactions involving currency and encompass the trade of commodities and services. A common practice among homesteaders is to engage in bartering within their community. This involves exchanging surplus crops, handcrafted crafts, or specialized talents for goods or services that satisfy their requirements. In addition to fostering a sense of interdependence throughout the community, this practice is consistent with the philosophy of self-sufficiency. Within the parameters of this discussion, the concept of financial sustainability becomes entangled with the idea of community resilience and the capacity to work together for mutual benefit.

The world of off-grid living is one in which frugality is a virtue and a practical need. When it comes to finances, it is essential to differentiate between requirements and wants and to make well-informed decisions regarding the distribution of resources. The homesteader acquires the ability to prioritize vital investments while simultaneously limiting expenses that are not necessary. Regarding the financial landscape of self-sufficient living, reusing and repurposing resources, adopting a Do-It-Yourself (DIY) philosophy, and embracing minimalism become essential components. When combined with resourcefulness, the capacity to live within one's means adds to financial security and the ability to be resilient in the face of unforeseen problems.

When it comes to off-grid life, it is essential to have a mindset that prioritizes self-sufficiency over consumerism to be financially prepared. The homesteader acquires the ability to question the necessity of purchases and frequently chooses sustainable, long-lasting ,and locally sourced alternatives whenever it is feasible. This adjustment in viewpoint aligns with the ideals of environmental sustainability and protects against the unneeded burden on the financial system. Financial considerations become linked with a more comprehensive philosophy of conscious living and responsible resource management when viewed in this light.

Despite the difficulties, the financial environment of off-grid life also offers one-of-a-kind chances for creative and innovative thinking. The homesteader transforms into an entrepreneur by cultivating not only crops and cattle but also marketable talents and goods. The concepts of self-sufficiency and environmental concern can be aligned with monetizing artisanal crafts, handcrafted goods, and sustainable activities. This can provide a source of revenue while also aligning with these principles. Therefore, to achieve financial success in off-grid living, it is necessary to possess finance expertise and a strong sense of entrepreneurial spirit.

Lifestyle Commitment

Relocating physically alone is not enough to achieve the profound and transforming lifestyle commitment needed for practical off-grid living. A change in perspective and a deliberate choice to adopt a way of life that emphasizes sustainability, self-sufficiency, and a stronger bond with the land are prerequisites for homesteading. It is more than just moving to a new place to live; it's a complete commitment to a way of life that calls for perseverance, devotion, and a deep comprehension of the responsibilities that come with independence.

The realization that off-grid living is a long-term project is at the core of the lifestyle commitment. In contrast to temporary lifestyle options, homesteading necessitates a commitment to a way of life that frequently entails laborious work, acclimating to a slower pace, and finding contentment in the routine duties of everyday living. This dedication goes beyond the idea's novelty to the day-to-day realities of tending to crops, caring for animals, and preserving vital infrastructure like energy and water. The homesteader must accept the cyclical nature of the seasons, the beat of the natural world, and the ups and downs of a way of life closely linked to the land.

Off-grid living entails adopting a mindset that emphasizes ingenuity and independence in addition to leaving behind the hustle and bustle of city life. The homesteader embraces a lifestyle that may be devoid of contemporary conveniences in an era when ease is frequently valued but makes up for it with a sense of accomplishment stemming from being able to support oneself. A greater appreciation for the food on the table, the warmth provided by a wood burner, and the energy obtained from the sun is fostered by this devotion. It gives the routine chores that keep the household running a purpose and turns them from meaningless into meaningful.

Moreover, committing to an off-grid lifestyle necessitates reassessing goals and beliefs. The homesteader deliberately puts necessities ahead of wants, concentrating on necessities rather than giving in to consumerist cravings. Resolving to live a simpler life requires giving up extra stuff and adopting a minimalist mindset. Living in harmony with the environment is making a conscious decision to lessen one's ecological impact and support the more general objective of environmental sustainability. This devotion comes with difficulties since it means redefining success beyond money gain and negotiating social expectations.

An essential component of the off-grid lifestyle is independence. The goal of the homesteader is to be independent of outside systems, such as the water and power systems and the networks that distribute food. As part of this dedication to independence, the skills required to meet basic requirements inside the homestead's boundaries must be developed. It necessitates knowledge about off-grid energy systems, water conservation strategies, and sustainable agriculture. The homesteader's dedication to independence becomes a source of pride as they design their sustainable ecosystem, making it more than just a practical requirement.

In addition, committing to an off-grid existence requires facing and overcoming obstacles. The homesteader must view obstacles as chances for development and education, regardless of whether they are brought on by inclement weather, malfunctioning equipment, or unanticipated setbacks. This dedication to resilience involves overcoming obstacles, actively looking for answers, and changing when faced with hardship. It's an attitude that turns failures into learning opportunities, promoting self-improvement and a feeling of achievement.

Off-grid living is intrinsically linked to a sense of community, even though it could be geographically scattered. The homesteader understands the benefits of forming relationships with people with similar ideals and struggles. This commitment entails contributing to a community network where resources are traded, expertise is shared, and assistance is easily accessible. Off-grid life fosters a strong feeling of community that serves as a safety net and a source of friendship and shared experiences, laying a solid foundation for the homesteader's journey.

Reevaluating the notion of time is another deliberate choice that comes with committing to a particular lifestyle. Off-grid living encourages people to adopt a more careful and attentive use of time in an era driven by rapid technological breakthroughs and the relentless quest for efficiency. The slower pace of rural living, the cyclical nature of the seasons, and the natural rhythms of day and night all become familiar to the homesteader. This dedication to a distinct temporality cultivates an enhanced awareness of life's cyclical nature and a strong bond with the environment.

Off-grid living also entails a lifestyle commitment to self-sufficiency beyond meeting basic physical requirements. It includes creating a balanced, all-encompassing life. The homesteader recognizes the value of a balanced lifestyle that provides for physical labor, intellectual stimulation, and times for introspection and actively participates in activities that support mental and emotional well-being. The homesteader's journey is about creating a meaningful and fulfilling existence, not just about surviving, thanks to the dedication to holistic self-sufficiency.

Finally, as lifestyle commitment shapes the fabric of the homesteader's journey, it is the cornerstone of successful off-grid living. It entails a significant change in perspective, a conscious decision to give sustainability, self-sufficiency, and a closer bond with the land priority. This long-term commitment calls for perseverance, devotion, and a readiness to face obstacles. It turns obstacles into opportunities, the ordinary into critical, and the homestead into a haven of independence and significance. Adopting an off-grid lifestyle means committing to a transformative journey beyond the homestead's physical borders and into personal development, community building, and peaceful coexistence with the natural world.

CHAPTER II

Location Selection

Factors Influencing Location Choice

One of the most critical decisions in the transition to off-grid life is choosing the proper location, and there are many different and complex considerations to consider. The place that a homesteader chooses involves more than just geography; it is an evaluation of all the factors that determine the feasibility and sustainability of an independent way of life. The choice of where to set up an off-grid homestead is complicated and requires careful analysis, considering everything from climate factors to regulatory issues, water supply, and legal restrictions.

The climate is one of the primary considerations when choosing an off-grid living place. Climates differ between locations, and each has advantages and disadvantages of its own. Temperature ranges, precipitation totals, and general weather patterns must all be considered by homesteaders. A successful off-grid experience requires a climate that fits the homesteader's preferences and the planned agricultural operations. For example, people who want growing seasons that last all year round may pick warmer locations, whereas people who want a mix of seasons may choose temperate regions. Planning for sustainable food production, energy requirements, and general comfort requires a thorough understanding of the nuances of local climates.

The features of the land and its topography are essential considerations when making decisions. The land must be suitable for building, farming, and other important uses. Careful consideration must be given to elements, including soil quality, slope, and the existence of natural resources like forests and water bodies. A homesteader looks for a place where the land can support their intended uses and provide opportunities for resource use. A carefully selected terrain makes building infrastructure more feasible, using environmentally friendly farming methods and peacefully coexisting with the surrounding area.

Water availability is a crucial consideration when choosing an off-grid homestead site. Water availability and quality are essential for many different uses, such as agriculture, raising animals, and meeting everyday needs in the home. The homesteader assesses the closeness of water sources, including lakes, rivers, and groundwater reserves. Furthermore, one must be thoroughly aware of local water rights and regulations to guarantee sustainable and lawful water usage. Not only does a site with readily available and dependable water resources make daily life easier, but it also lays the groundwork for long-term homestead sustainability.

Regulations play a significant role when deciding whether to live off the grid. RulesLocal, state, and federal regulations can significantly affect homesteaders' capacity to start and sustain an independent way of life. Land-use restrictions, building codes, and zoning laws specify what activities are allowed in a specific location. The homesteader searches for a place that fits their idea of off-grid living while navigating these regulatory frameworks to ensure compliance. Comprehending and adhering to legislative limitations is essential for fostering a cordial rapport with local authorities and ensuring a sustainable, extended homesteading journey.

One more consideration that affects location selection is accessibility to necessary services. Off-grid life is motivated by the desire for independence and seclusion, but pragmatic concerns demand moderation. The availability of healthcare, emergency services, and educational resources may influence where to build a homestead. The advantages of being isolated must be balanced against the necessity of periodically accessing essential services for the homesteader. Finding this balance guarantees that the site selected permits a certain degree of self-sufficiency while offering necessary assistance when required.

The viability of an off-grid location is largely dependent on energy issues. Crucial elements impacting this choice are the amount of sunshine available for solar power, wind patterns for wind energy, and the possibility of other renewable sources. To achieve energy independence, a homesteader determines whether using natural resources to generate electricity is feasible. For an off-grid homestead to succeed in the long run, it is essential to comprehend the local energy landscape, potential barriers to adopting renewable energy, and the sustainability of the chosen area of energy use.

Aspects of the community and culture play a significant role in the entire off-grid living experience and impact place selection. A community that upholds similar ideals views sustainability and is open to accepting the difficulties of independent life, which may be what the homesteader is looking for. Cultural congruence, encompassing local practices and traditions, might improve the homesteader's feeling of acceptance and assimilation into the community. This social component of place selection is essential for individuals who desire community support and interpersonal relationships in an off-grid lifestyle.

The process of making decisions also takes economic factors into account. The viability of off-grid living depends on several factors, including the cost of land, the availability of jobs, and the general financial stability of the selected area. The homesteader needs to assess if there are chances for income production in case they become necessary and whether the local economy supports their goal of self-sufficiency. A thorough examination of economic variables guarantees that the site selection aligns with the financial requirements of living off the grid, promoting a long-lasting and satisfying experience.

One of the main factors impacting location selection is the accessibility of resources for sustainable living. A place with plenty of natural resources, such as timber, wildlife, and healthy soil, is what a homesteader looks for. Access to these resources helps the homestead achieve its sustainable building, agriculture, and general self-sufficiency objectives. The homestead can prosper without compromising the environment if resources are used responsibly, which requires understanding the local ecology and how resilient it is to human activity.

In summary, many different and related factors affect where people live off the grid. A thorough assessment of the climate, geography, availability of water, regulatory frameworks, accessibility to services, energy considerations, cultural compatibility, economic aspects, and resource availability is undertaken by the homesteader. This all-encompassing strategy guarantees that the site selection aligns with the goals of sustainability, self-sufficiency, and a closer relationship with the land. The location of an off-grid homestead is a complex decision that calls for a careful balancing act between pragmatic issues, individual preferences, and a dedication to an independent and environmentally conscious way of life.

Climate Considerations

When making decisions about going off the grid, climate is one of the most important factors to take into account. The viability, comfort, and sustainability of an independent lifestyle are significantly impacted by the climate of a chosen place. Homesteaders, empowered by their understanding and adaptation to their chosen place's unique weather patterns, temperature ranges, and seasonal variations, thrive, unlike urban people who may take a stable climate for granted.

The temperature range encountered year-round is the primary factor to consider when deciding whether to live off the grid when it comes to climate. The temperature profiles of different areas vary greatly, from bitter cold to intense heat. Warmer climates may be better for growers who want a growing season that lasts all year round since they enable longer agricultural seasons. On the other hand, people who prefer a balance of different seasons can choose to live in temperate regions where they can enjoy the splendor of spring, summer, fall, and winter. The success of an off-grid lifestyle for homesteaders is largely dependent on their capacity to adjust to and prosper in the temperature extremes of the place they have selected, a feat that brings immense satisfaction.

An important factor in off-grid climatic considerations is precipitation patterns. The volume and distribution of snowfall or rainfall affects the water available for everyday home requirements, animals, and crops. Certain farming practices may be more successful in areas with regular rainfall, whereas areas with more erratic precipitation may require more sophisticated methods of collecting and storing water. The homesteader evaluates the local precipitation patterns thoroughly, comprehends seasonal fluctuations, and plans water management techniques appropriately. The homestead's resistance to shifting weather patterns is significantly influenced by its capacity to use and preserve its water resources, providing a sense of security in the face of unpredictable weather.

Seasonal changes, which are frequently more noticeable in some regions, add another level of complexity to the planning of homesteaders. For example, the melting of the earth during the winter-spring transition can affect gardening and construction activities. Cold winters may call for extra heating systems and insulation preparations to ensure comfort and safety. Comprehending these seasonal subtleties is essential for modifying farming methods, overseeing energy resources, and being fully equipped to face the obstacles posed by the varying seasons. Recognizing the interdependence of the annual cycle and adjusting to particular seasons is part of a holistic approach to climate considerations.

Another critical factor in determining the climate for off-grid life is wind patterns. The wind can influence both the stability of structures and the energy generated by wind turbines. Construction and energy infrastructure planning must be done carefully in coastal areas and areas vulnerable to severe winds. Furthermore, wind patterns affect how people perceive temperature and may raise the possibility of flames in some areas. When selecting a site, the homesteader considers these elements, ensuring that the location will allow them to tolerate wind exposure and utilize it as a renewable energy source.

Altitude is a factor that has its advantages and disadvantages and is frequently linked to climate. Lower temperatures are more common at higher elevations, which may impact crop selection and the total amount of energy needed for heating. Higher altitudes' oxygen content may affect both human and animal health. The homesteader has to ensure the chosen site supports a prosperous off-grid lifestyle by carefully considering the impact of altitude on everyday life, crops, and infrastructure.

Homesteaders must plan by having a thorough understanding of the microclimates that exist within a broader region. Microclimates are localized weather patterns impacted by topography, water bodies, and flora. In a mountainous environment, a valley may get varying amounts of precipitation and have different temperatures than the surrounding terrain. The homesteader carefully plans the placement of particular activities by considering these microclimates. For example, placing dwellings in locations protected from inclement weather guarantees comfort and safety, while planting crops in regions with ideal microclimates can increase agricultural productivity.

Anticipating extreme weather events, such as storms, hurricanes, or droughts, is another aspect of climate considerations. Since these occurrences differ in intensity and frequency between areas, the homesteader needs to evaluate the danger and make plans appropriately. Developing emergency plans, conserving water during droughts, and erecting weather-resistant buildings are all essential components of climate considerations. It takes more than simply infrastructure to withstand these extremes; homesteaders' adaptation and foresight make them resilient.

Furthermore, taking climate change into account takes environmental sustainability in a larger framework, in addition to its immediate effects on day-to-day living into account. Homesteaders try to leave as little of an ecological imprint as possible since they understand how intertwined climatic and environmental systems are. Sustainable farming methods, resource conservation, and ethical waste disposal align with the homesteader's dedication to environmental stewardship. The homesteader ensures long-term sustainability by establishing a healthy relationship with the natural environment by selecting a location that benefits from these practices.

In summary, climate is a critical factor in the decision-making process for off-grid living. The area that a homesteader chooses has a significant impact on their capacity to adapt, flourish, and maintain a self-sufficient existence. Each aspect of the local climate, including temperature ranges, precipitation patterns, wind exposure, altitude, and microclimates, must be carefully considered. A proficient homesteader approaches these factors from an all-encompassing standpoint, understanding how climate affects crops, energy, buildings, and general well-being. People who choose an off-grid existence that respects and coexists with nature while also being in line with their preferences and needs are paving the way for a climate-conscious lifestyle.

Legal and Regulatory Aspects

When considering whether to go off the grid, legal and regulatory considerations are the most critical factors in their decision-making process. Geographical and climatic factors are not the only factors that influence the placement of an independent homestead; local, state, and federal laws have a significant role in determining what is allowed on the selected plot of land. For the homesteader, navigating the intricate web of land use, building, and zoning restrictions becomes crucial since it affects not just the viability of their vision but also the long-term sustainability of their off-grid existence.

What can be done in a particular location depends on zoning laws, which divide land into several use zones. There are rules specific to residential, agricultural, commercial, and industrial zones. The homesteader needs to ensure that their proposed land uses comply with the approved land use by carefully reviewing the zoning laws of possible places. While some areas may have stricter regulations that restrict the possibilities of off-grid living, others may have more liberal zoning laws that permit a wider variety of activities. To maintain good relations with local government and steer clear of any legal issues, it is essential to comprehend and abide by zoning laws.

Building codes are a body of laws that specify the requirements for infrastructure and building practices. They include environmental factors, safety features, and structural integrity. Homesteaders must follow these rules to guarantee that their homes and buildings are secure, long-lasting, and ecologically conscious. Striking a balance between adhering to safety regulations and maintaining the independence and distinctiveness of off-grid housing presents a difficulty. To create structures that comply with sustainability and self-sufficiency while meeting regulatory criteria, working within the constraints of building regulations demands ingenuity and inventiveness.

Land-use rules further shape homesteaders' options for using the selected property. These rules can forbid particular pursuits or prescribe specific land management methods. For example, wildlife conservation, wetland preservation, or deforestation limitations may affect the homesteader's intentions for infrastructure expansion or agriculture. A responsible homesteader assesses land-use laws to ensure their methods satisfy their self-sufficiency requirements and environmental protection aims.

Legal and regulatory issues frequently impact access to utilities. There may be limitations on the homesteader's ability to connect to the municipal water supply or electrical grid in some areas. This constraint requires the creation of water collection technologies and alternate energy sources. Rules governing sewage systems and waste disposal also apply; off-grid solutions, such as composting toilets and greywater management, are frequently the best choices. It is essential to navigate these legal and regulatory obstacles to create a self-sufficient farmhouse without conventional utility services.

Homesteaders occasionally come across off-grid or alternative building regulations designed to meet the unique requirements and goals of individuals seeking a self-sufficient lifestyle. These standards offer recommendations that promote creativity and sustainability while acknowledging the unique qualities of off-grid life. Communities that adopt off-grid lifestyles may create laws to encourage and support the development of an independent way of life. Establishing such regulations by proactively engaging with communities and local authorities can result in a legislative environment supporting off-grid life.

Comprehending property rights, land ownership, and any constraints homeowners' organizations impose are essential to navigating legal and regulatory elements. Certain regions might impose limitations on land usage or architectural designs, whereas other areas might enforce covenants that affect the homesteader's capacity to carry out specific activities. Understanding property rights and associated restrictions is critical to prevent legal issues and ensure that the chosen site permits the level of autonomy desired in off-grid life.

Permits and environmental impact assessments are additional factors to consider when navigating the legal landscape of off-grid life. Some operations may need permits to ensure that environmental standards are followed, such as removing land, using water, or building in environmentally sensitive areas. To acquire the required permits, the homesteader must interact with the appropriate authorities and show they are committed to practicing responsible land stewardship. A sustainable and environmentally accountable off-grid farm requires legal attention, which includes navigating the bureaucratic maze of environmental evaluations.

Homesteaders need to think about state and federal legislation that could affect their lifestyle choices in addition to local regulations. For instance, state laws frequently govern water rights, and comprehension of these laws is essential to sustainable water management. Federal rules could be relevant when doing things like producing renewable energy. Adhering to these regulations guarantees that the homesteader functions within the broader legal structure and promotes an eco-friendly and self-sufficient way of life.

Difficulties could occur when legislative and regulatory frameworks are not explicitly created to support off-grid life. In these situations, homesteaders can find themselves pushing for modifications to the laws as they stand or collaborating with the local government to create new strategies. To advocate for off-grid living, it is frequently necessary to inform legislators about its unique qualities and advantages while emphasizing its potential benefits for community resilience, sustainable development, and environmental conservation.

Off-grid living's legal and regulatory features offer

chances for participation and cooperation in addition to problems. The homesteader actively participates in local governance, helping shape laws that uphold sustainability and self-sufficiency. Developing a good rapport with community stakeholders, environmental organizations, and local government officials is essential to raising awareness and gaining support for off-grid living. In addition to making legal compliance easier, this cooperative method helps the community accept off-grid living more widely.

In conclusion, those considering an off-grid lifestyle

must consider the legal and regulatory implications. Regulations about zoning, construction, land use, and environmental assessments influence the viability and endurance of the homesteader's concept. It takes diligence, ingenuity, and a willingness to interact with local, state, and federal authorities to navigate complex legal environments successfully. Successful homesteaders actively contribute to creating legislative frameworks that recognize and support the distinctive qualities of off-grid living and abiding by current restrictions. Through comprehension, negotiation, and active participation in the legal environment.

CHAPTER III

Building Your Homestead

Planning and Design

An off-grid homestead—a carefully planned concept of sustainable living, self-sufficiency, and harmony with nature—requires planning and design. From structural architecture to renewable energy system integration, every aspect of planning and design affects off-grid living practicality and longevity. This complex procedure considers the homesteader's demands, environmental conditions, and dedication to a sustainable and harmonious homestead.

An off-grid homestead's planning must consider the homesteader's goals, resources, and location. The first step is understanding the goals—sustainable agriculture, animal husbandry, or renewable energy. Homesteaders plan the arrangement of buildings, gardens, and infrastructure to enhance efficiency and functionality. Water management is crucial to planning. The homesteader studies water sources, including wells and catchment systems, and plans for effective distribution and conservation. To guarantee sustainable homestead water use, irrigation, rainwater harvesting, and greywater recycling systems must be carefully designed. Water management tactics are improved by permaculture principles like contouring the soil to capture and direct water flow.

Renewable energy sources are prioritized in the planning phase to power the homestead. Local climate, terrain, and energy needs determine evaluations of solar, wind, and micro-hydro systems. The homesteader wants passive solar design to maximize natural heating and cooling in structures. The homestead's energy use should be sustainable and minimize its environmental impact.

Off-grid living requires a waste management strategy. Homesteaders develop composting, recycling, and responsible non-recyclable waste systems. The design incorporates conscientious consumption and sustainable packaging to reduce waste. Off-grid composting toilets turn human waste into beneficial compost, turning a stressful task into a regenerative process.

Structures on the homestead are designed for usefulness and environmental effect. Energy efficiency is improved via passive solar architecture, such as positioning buildings to utilize sunlight. Construction decreases ecological impact and connects to the landscape using natural, locally available materials. Cob or straw bale construction can help the homesteader meet sustainability goals and create a distinctive and attractive design.

Homesteaders consider food and medicinal plant cultivation during planning. Gardens and orchards follow permaculture design principles, emphasizing sustainable and self-sufficient agriculture. Mulching, companion planting, and water-efficient irrigation strengthen the agricultural ecology. The goal is to produce a diverse, regenerative landscape that supports biodiversity, soil health, and homesteader nourishment.

Planning and designing for livestock integration is also essential. The homesteader assesses animal needs, organizes efficient and sustainable animal husbandry, and builds barns and coops for shelter and protection. Livestock help with soil fertility, insect control, and homestead resilience, creating a healthy environment. The design of off-grid systems includes communication and connectivity. Homesteaders seek independence from traditional utilities, but being connected is essential. To ensure remote connectivity, satellite internet, and two-way radio are integrated into the architecture. Homestead design balances self-sufficiency with information and community participation by including emergency communication plans and ways to stay updated about local and global affairs.

Homesteaders anticipate future expansion and change during planning. Scalability and adaptability are possible with design flexibility. The homestead design should adapt to changing circumstances, such as increasing agricultural operations, renewable energy sources, or family size. A good plan anticipates changes and supports continual improvement and sustainability.

Transitioning from planning to implementation requires careful homestead design execution. Building structures, constructing renewable energy systems, or implementing water management infrastructure requires practical skills and imaginative problem-solving. The homesteader may use self-taught skills, advice from other homesteaders, and professional help to complete many of these undertakings.

Homesteaders living off-grid are encouraged to DIY. Building a rainwater collection system, composting toilets, or solar panels by hand promotes self-sufficiency and resourcefulness. DIY projects allow homesteaders to take charge of their lifestyle, feel accomplished, and connect with the homestead.

Implementation requires fitting the homestead design to the location. Unexpected issues like soil quality, water availability, or wildlife interactions may need plan revisions. The homesteader must be flexible and inventive at this phase because adaptability is part of the design process.

Off-grid homesteads require regular maintenance and improvement. The Homesteader regularly assesses wear and tear, updates systems, and incorporates past lessons. This iterative design process keeps the homestead dynamic, flexible, and aligned with the homesteader's changing requirements and goals.

Community involvement is also essential in off-grid planning and design. Homesteaders may join local homesteading groups or work with neighbors who share their values. Sharing knowledge, resources, and support strengthens the off-grid community. Beyond its physical borders, the homestead design includes relationships and networks that create belonging and shared purpose.

In conclusion, off-grid homestead success depends on planning and design, which includes water and energy management, waste disposal, agricultural techniques, and infrastructure layout. A careful approach that mixes sustainability, self-sufficiency, and a solid connection to nature realizes the homesteader's ideal. The off-grid homestead's dynamic and resilient lifestyle of harmony with nature, ingenuity, and the pursuit of a sustainable and meaningful existence is maintained by planning, implementation, and adaptability.

Construction Basics

The foundation of an off-grid farmhouse is construction, which turns an idea into a physical reality. Adherence to ecological principles, inventiveness, and practical abilities are all required during construction. Building homes and setting up water, energy, and waste management systems are examples of homesteaders' hands-on approach, reflecting the values of resilience and self-sufficiency. Regarding off-grid living, construction fundamentals cover various factors, such as choosing suitable building materials, implementing energy-efficient designs, and encouraging a harmonious coexistence with the surrounding environment.

Selecting the building materials is a crucial step when building off the grid. Locally produced and sustainable products lessen the homestead's ecological imprint and align with environmental stewardship concepts. Materials that provide insulation and sustainability include straw bales, adobe, cob, and timber from responsibly managed forests. Utilizing recovered or recycled materials increases the environmentally friendly element of the building by maximizing resource utilization and reducing waste. When choosing materials, the homesteader takes the desired area's terrain and climate into account to ensure the materials are appropriate for the local environment and enhance the overall energy efficiency of the structures.

Applying passive solar design concepts is one of the most important factors to consider while building off the grid. By optimizing the use of sunlight to heat and cool buildings naturally, this design method lessens the need for external energy sources. A more comfortable and energy-efficient atmosphere can be achieved by orienting structures to receive as much sun exposure as possible in the winter and providing shade in the summer. Large windows and thermal mass components, such as stone walls or earthen flooring, absorb and retain heat, which control inside temperatures and improve sustainability overall.

Do-it-yourself (DIY) building methods are frequently used to construct off-grid homes, which reflects the homesteader's dedication to actively participating in the building process. Acquiring hands-on construction knowledge becomes essential to living off the grid. The homesteader embraces a combination of self-taught expertise, advice from seasoned builders, and, when necessary, professional aid when it comes to framing walls, roofing, and flooring. This do-it-yourself mentality encourages a sense of pride and ownership in the built environment and allows homesteaders to change their living areas actively.

A crucial component of building off the grid is installing water management infrastructure, which entails installing systems for gathering, storing, and distributing water. Rainwater harvesting is a popular off-grid homesteading technique that involves gathering rain from rooftops and storing it in tanks. The homesteader considers gutter systems, filtering mechanisms, and roof materials while designing an effective rainwater collection and storage system. Water-efficient fixtures and plumbing systems distribute water for irrigation and domestic use, promoting responsible water use across the property.

Solutions for waste management are equally crucial to off-grid buildings. The ecological method of waste disposal is best demonstrated by composting toilets, which turn human waste into nutrient-rich compost. Water conservation is aided by greywater systems, which are made to recycle and utilize domestic wastewater. A homesteader's capacity to reduce waste output and recycle materials is further improved by building compost bins and sorting stations. A dedication to conscientious and regenerative processes is demonstrated by incorporating these waste management techniques into the overall construction plan.

A key component of off-grid building is energy infrastructure, which focuses on utilizing renewable energy sources to supply the homestead with electricity. Solar energy is captured and transformed into power by solar panels installed on rooftops or ground-mounted arrays. An additional renewable energy source is provided by wind turbines, which are positioned to capture prevailing winds. Micro-hydro systems that use water flow are appropriate for places with a supply of flowing water. The homesteader meticulously plans the installation of these systems, considering local climate, seasonal fluctuations, and energy requirements. Including energy-saving lighting and appliances further improves the off-grid energy infrastructure's sustainability.

Off-grid energy system construction frequently combines do-it-yourself work with expert guidance. The homesteader learns about electrical wiring, battery storage, and system design to guarantee the successful application of renewable energy sources. In certain instances, seeking advice from proficient off-grid energy specialists can be imperative to enhance the system's dependability and efficiency. The intention is to create an energy infrastructure that will serve the homestead's present needs and future expansion and evolving energy demands.

More construction work is required on the off-grid homestead to accommodate cattle. When constructing barns, coops, and shelters, it's essential to keep the animals' safety from the weather, well-being, and optimal use of space in mind. The homesteader incorporates waste management systems, ventilation, and natural lighting into the construction of their buildings to support sustainable animal husbandry techniques. The structure of enclosures and fencing adds even more to the livestock regions' general usefulness and safety. These fundamental off-grid homestead components are built with the requirements of animals and sustainability in mind.

The off-grid design considers practical considerations, aesthetics, and interaction with the surrounding environment. Homesteaders establish a healthy interaction between their buildings and the surrounding environment to prevent upsetting the natural ecology. Native plant plantings, applying permaculture design concepts, and land contouring to improve water retention are landscaping techniques that will enhance the homestead's overall aesthetic appeal and ecological balance. This sense of unity and interconnectedness is fostered by the artificial world being an extension of the natural landscape.

During the building phase, obstacles could appear, forcing the homesteader to adjust and find quick fixes. Changes to the topography, unforeseen weather, or the identification of less-than-ideal soil quality could require modifying the original construction schedule. Resilience and inventiveness in overcoming these obstacles are essential components of a well-executed off-grid building project. The homesteader adopts a philosophy of constant improvement, drawing lessons from each building effort and using those lessons in subsequent undertakings.

The off-grid building also involves community involvement, with the homesteader frequently participating in neighborhood-building networks or exchanging knowledge with like-minded people. In the off-grid community, cooperation promotes resource sharing, skill sharing, and support among members. Participating in the community improves the collective knowledge and resilience of the off-grid lifestyle, whether helping with construction projects or looking for advice from seasoned builders.

To sum up, the fundamentals of construction are the cornerstone of off-grid living, turning the homesteader's dream into a livable and sustainable reality. Every facet of construction, from the choice of ecologically friendly building materials to the application of energy-efficient designs and the integration of water, waste, and energy management systems, displays the dedication to resilience and self-sufficiency. The do-it-yourself mentality, practical approach, and capacity for problem-solving exhibited by homesteaders are factors that make off-grid building projects successful. In establishing a peaceful and replenishing habitat, the homesteader builds tangible structures and molds a way of life based on creativity, sustainability, and a close relationship with the natural world.

Sustainable Building Practices

Responsible and eco-conscious construction relies on sustainable approaches to reduce environmental impact, improve resource efficiency, and develop robust, naturally harmonious structures. Off-grid living emphasizes self-sufficiency and environmental responsibility, making sustainable building practices necessary for every construction. Homesteaders promote environmental and human health in material selection, energy efficiency, and waste management.

Sustainable building starts with material selection. Traditional building uses resource-intensive materials like concrete and steel, which increase carbon emissions and environmental deterioration. In contrast, sustainable building uses renewable, local, and low- impact materials. Responsible timber harvesting from well-managed forests provides a renewable construction resource. Natural materials like adobe, cob, and straw bales insulate well and reduce carbon emissions. Recycled wood and metal minimize waste and provide individuality to the built environment.

Sustainable building approaches emphasize energy efficiency, especially in off-grid construction when energy is generated and managed on-site. Optimizing structure orientation to capture sunlight for winter heating and shading components to prevent summer heat gain are critical to passive solar design. Well-insulated buildings with high thermal mass, heat-storing, and heat-releasing materials maintain a steady indoor climate without excessive heating or cooling. Energy-efficient windows and doors improve insulation, lowering energy use.

Sustainable off-grid building uses renewable energy. Solar panels carefully placed capture sunlight and generate electricity. Wind turbines create energy in places with constant wind patterns. Micro-hydro systems generate electricity from water. Homesteaders can lessen their dependence on non-renewable energy and promote self-sufficiency and environmental responsibility by incorporating these renewable energy sources into their construction plans.

Sustainable building practices emphasize water efficiency, conservation, and disposal. Rooftop rainwater gathering systems supply sustainable water. Greywater systems utilize sink, shower, and washing machine wastewater, saving freshwater. Low-flow toilets and aerated faucets help conserve water. Landscape swales and other water-harvesting structures improve water retention and reduce runoff, promoting regenerative water management.

Waste reduction and responsible disposal are essential to sustainable building. Packaging, unused building materials, and construction trash are abundant. The "reduce, reuse, recycle" technique reduces construction's environmental impact. Sustainability includes salvaging and repurposing resources from destroyed constructions, using recycled or upcycled materials, and recycling or composting garbage. Materials are carefully obtained, used efficiently, and diverted from landfills through responsible waste management throughout construction.

Sustainable construction approaches use passive cooling and ventilation to save energy and improve comfort. Natural ventilation from strategically positioned windows and vents circulates fresh air without mechanical conditioning. Buildings with proper insulation, ventilation, and shading to limit direct sunlight reduce heat gain and air conditioning use. Slowly absorbing and releasing heat, thermal mass materials like stone or earthen flooring lower indoor temperatures.

Construction with green or living roofs has environmental benefits. Vegetation on green roofs insulates and reduces heat absorption. They absorb and reduce precipitation runoff, helping regulate stormwater. Green roofs promote ecological diversity in the built environment by providing habitats for birds, insects, and other species. Beyond their essential benefits, green roofs beautify and regenerate sustainable dwellings.

Sustainable construction optimizes building orientation with the sun's path to capture natural light and heat. Correctly oriented buildings maximize winter sunshine, reducing the need for artificial heating. In summer, overhangs and deciduous trees block direct sunlight, improving cooling effectiveness. Carefully positioning windows and openings maximizes natural light and ventilation, making the home comfortable and energy-efficient.

Non-toxic coatings improve indoor air quality and occupant health. Sustainable building approaches use low- or no-VOC materials to clean indoor air. Natural finishes like clay plaster or lime wash promote indoor health and eco-friendly building.

These treatments offer visual variety without the environmental effect of chemical alternatives. Community engagement and knowledge-sharing are critical to sustainable building. Homesteaders join local building networks, work with like-minded people, and share their experiences. This collaborative method promotes learning, innovation, and resource exchange in sustainable building. Homesteaders join a network that spreads sustainable techniques by helping with construction, conducting workshops, or supporting local building projects.

Sustainable building practices underpinning responsible and eco-conscious off-grid construction. Renewable and locally produced materials, energy-efficient design, water conservation, and waste management demonstrate environmental care and self-sufficiency. Sustainable construction is a comprehensive perspective that covers material selection, energy consumption, water management, and waste disposal throughout a structure's existence. The homesteader creates a resilient and regenerative living environment with these techniques and joins a global movement toward more sustainable and harmonious building and living.

CHAPTER IV

Off-Grid Energy Solutions

Solar Power

Solar power, captured from the sun's plentiful energy, has revolutionized renewable energy. Solar power symbolizes independence from utility grids in off-grid living, where self-sufficiency and sustainability are vital. Solar panels allow homesteaders to power their dwellings, satisfy energy needs, and live an environmentally responsible lifestyle. This section discusses solar power's technology, applications, benefits, drawbacks, and impact on off-grid life.

Solar power uses photovoltaic (PV) cells to turn sunlight into electricity. Silicon, a photovoltaic semiconductor, is used to make these cells. Solar radiation excites electrons in solar cells, providing an electric current. Inverters convert DC to AC, making it compatible with residential and office electrical systems. Solar panels are modular, so homesteaders can scale their solar power systems to suit energy needs.

Living off-grid often means being disconnected from utilities. In such cases, solar electricity is essential for daily energy needs. Homesteaders deliberately place solar panels on rooftops, ground-mounted arrays, or other sites to capture daytime sunshine. Battery storage provides a steady power source even on overcast or nocturnal days. This ability to store solar energy solves one of the problems of intermittent renewable sources, allowing energy production autonomy.

Solar power has uses beyond domestic electricity in off-grid life. Solar water heaters heat domestic water using sunshine, minimizing dependence on existing techniques. Sunlight-powered ovens and cookers are an eco-friendly alternative to stoves. These applications show how solar power can be used for various off-grid uses. Homesteaders can use energy sustainably by integrating solar technologies into daily life.

The many benefits of solar power in off-grid living have made it popular in the self-sufficiency movement. Environmental impact reduction is a significant benefit. Solar electricity is clean, renewable, and emits less greenhouse gas than fossil fuels. Homesteaders reduce their carbon footprint and climate change by using solar energy. Due to its decentralization, solar electricity requires less energy transportation infrastructure, reducing environmental impacts.

Economic factors support off-grid solar power. Solar panels and equipment cost a lot, yet they save money over time. Homesteaders can reduce or eliminate their monthly electricity expenses depending on the size and effectiveness of their solar power system. Many states and municipal governments give incentives, rebates, or tax credits to encourage the adoption of solar technology, making the switch more affordable for off-grid aficionados.

Solar power gives off-grid residents energy independence. Homesteaders can escape utility service disruptions by generating their electricity. This self-reliance fits off-grid living's emphasis on autonomy and resilience in satisfying fundamental requirements. Creating and storing energy on-site gives off-grid residences a reliable power source.

Solar power systems are appealing for off-grid living due to their inexpensive upkeep. Solar panels last a long time and require little maintenance. Regular dust removal, component checks, and battery maintenance are enough to keep a solar power system running smoothly. This differs from typical utility services and other energy generators requiring constant maintenance and service disruptions.

Solar panels beautify off-grid dwellings as well as function. Modern solar arrays blend into many architectural forms, adding beauty to the built environment. Off-grid construction projects that use solar technologies show a dedication to sustainability and environmental responsibility, making solar panels symbols of a thoughtful and forward-thinking lifestyle.

Despite its benefits, off-grid solar electricity has drawbacks. Sunlight variations due to weather, time of day, and seasonal changes are a significant issue. Cloudy days or prolonged rain can limit solar panel efficiency and energy production. Homesteaders employ energy storage systems like batteries to store excess energy during peak sunshine hours for usage during low sunlight.

Solar panel installation is complicated due to logistics and space. Off-grid dwellings may have limited solar panel space in highly forested or gloomy places. Solar panel direction and tilt affect efficiency. Thus, planning is needed to maximize sunshine exposure. Innovative technologies like flexible mounting systems or sun trackers can improve solar panel performance but may increase system complexity and expense.

Sustainability also considers the environmental impact of solar panel manufacturing and disposal. Solar panels operate cleanly and sustainably, but their creation requires extracting and processing silicon, metals, and other raw materials. Recycling and eco-friendly materials are being used to make solar panels more sustainable. Recycling and sustainable manufacturing will help address these issues as the sector evolves.

Innovations in solar technology boost efficiency, cost, and versatility. Thin-film solar cells, organic solar cells, and solar paint enable solar power integration into more surfaces and structures. These developments may solve some problems with standard solar panels, opening new options for off-grid solar energy use. As research and development continue, off-grid solar electricity may become more accessible and sustainable.

Finally, solar power is essential for self-sufficient homesteaders, providing clean, renewable, and adaptable energy. Beyond power generation, the technology can heat water, cook, and meet other demands, demonstrating its full role in sustainable living. Solar power's environmental, economic, and energy independence benefits make it popular among off-grid residents. Technological advances and a commitment to sustainability will overcome problems, reinforcing solar power's role as a facilitator of off-grid life. Solar power inspires people and communities to live harmoniously with the environment.

Wind Energy

Wind energy, derived from air kinetic energy, is a significant participant in the global transition to renewable and sustainable energy. Wind energy can replace conventional power sources in off-grid living, where independence and environmental care are vital. Wind turbines allow homesteaders to create energy, lessen their dependence on utility systems, and live sustainably. This section examines the complex technology of wind energy, its applications, benefits, drawbacks, and dramatic impact on off-grid living.

Wind turbines, the leading wind energy source, convert air kinetic energy into mechanical energy and electricity. A conventional wind turbine has hub-mounted rotor blades on a tall tower. Wind spins rotor blades, powering a generator. The modular structure of wind turbines allows homesteaders to scale their turbine size and quantity dependent on energy needs and wind conditions.

Wind is a stable supply in off-grid living areas.

Homesteaders optimize energy production by positioning wind turbines for prevailing winds. Wind power can mitigate the intermittent nature of renewable energy sources like solar power. Homesteaders improve off-grid power reliability and sustainability with hybrid systems that combine wind and solar energy.

Wind energy has more uses than electricity in off-grid

life: wind turbines power irrigation water pumps, a sustainable agricultural option. Wind energy may desalinate water in off-grid areas, easing water scarcity. These applications demonstrate wind energy's adaptability as a power source and off-grid alternative. Homesteaders may use energy sustainably by integrating wind technologies into daily life.

A significant benefit of wind energy is its continuous

electricity generation. Unlike solar power, wind energy is reliable since it may be used day and night. Many off-grid areas, especially those with vast landscapes and elevated terrain, provide continuous wind resources despite wind speed and direction variations. Off-grid power systems are more stable and resilient with this reliability.

Economic factors support wind energy in off-grid living. Wind turbines have high upfront expenses but high long-term financial rewards. Wind turbines last longer and cost less to operate and maintain. Homesteaders can eliminate monthly energy payments by installing wind turbines to provide reliable, cost-effective electricity. Many governments and local authorities give incentives, subsidies, or tax credits to encourage wind energy use, making it affordable for off-grid enthusiasts.

Wind energy reduces greenhouse gas emissions and non-renewable resource use, helping off-grid living achieve environmental goals. Wind turbines lessen the ecological impact of fossil fuel power generation. Homesteaders can lower their carbon footprint and mitigate climate change by capturing wind power. Wind energy's decentralization reduces energy transportation infrastructure and ecological disruptions, supporting environmental responsibility.

Off-grid life benefits from wind energy's energy independence. Wind turbines allow homesteaders to generate their electricity. This autonomy makes off-grid dwellings more resilient, maintaining a steady power supply even in remote areas. Off-grid living emphasizes self-sufficiency and independence, and wind energy on-site provides a constant power supply.

Wind turbines have a lower environmental impact than other energy sources. The land beneath and surrounding wind turbines can be used for agriculture, avoiding ecosystem impact. The ecological effects of wind farms are further reduced by their smaller footprints than power stations. Off-grid homesteaders who value sustainability and harmony with nature may find wind energy appealing.

In off-grid life, wind energy has many benefits but also drawbacks. Wind speed and direction variability is a significant issue. Wind turbine efficiency depends on constant wind patterns. Therefore, low or unexpected wind speeds may not be ideal for wind energy generation. Homesteaders must carefully examine local wind conditions and do feasibility studies to establish the potential of wind energy.

Wind turbines' visual and acoustic effects are another issue. Some may find gently whirling turbines attractive, but others may find them intrusive. In areas where dwellings are near turbines, whirling blades, and mechanical components can make noise. Planning and community interaction are needed to balance wind energy with landscape visual and aural qualities.

Maintenance is essential for wind energy systems to work well and last. Moving parts must be lubricated, and electrical components must be checked regularly to prevent failures and fix faults quickly. Maintaining off-grid homes is complicated by their distance. Homesteaders must be prepared to handle maintenance issues in an off-grid situation when inspecting and repairing turbines.

The environmental impact of wind energy infrastructure's manufacture, transporting, and decommissioning is also considered. Wind turbine materials like steel and rare earth metals for magnets are mined and processed, which can harm the environment. However, the industry is working to make production processes more sustainable and reduce environmental effects. A closed-loop system that reduces waste and ecological disruption requires wind turbine decommissioning and recycling.

Advances in wind turbine technology are addressing wind energy concerns. Design, materials, and manufacturing innovations boost efficiency, reliability, and sustainability. Quieter turbines, new blade designs, and modular components make wind energy systems more adaptable to varied surroundings and community preferences. Research and development will help solve problems and improve off-grid wind energy performance as the market evolves.

Alternative Power Sources

The search for environmentally friendly and sustainable energy solutions has centered on alternative power sources, particularly when it comes to off-grid living. Apart from utility-based electricity, many alternative power sources have evolved to suit people's energy demands and provide them with more autonomy and resilience. These substitutes utilize inventive technologies, renewable energy sources, and the environment to deliver dependable off-grid power options. This section examines several alternative power sources, looking at their underlying technology, uses, benefits, drawbacks, and overall effect on changing the face of energy independence.

Biomass energy, produced from organic resources like wood and agricultural waste, is one well-known alternative power source. Heat is released during biomass combustion and can be utilized directly for heating or transformed into electrical power. For off-grid living in areas with plentiful access to wood and agricultural leftovers, biomass power is especially pertinent. Because biomass systems are decentralized, homesteaders can produce energy locally and become less reliant on outside sources. Furthermore, biomass is a sustainable substitute because the amount of carbon dioxide emitted after combustion is nearly equivalent to the amount absorbed by the plants during growth.

Hydropower is another well-known option that produces electricity by harnessing the energy of flowing water. Micro-hydro systems use tiny water flows to power turbines and generate electricity, making them ideal for off-grid applications. Homesteaders frequently incorporate micro-hydro systems into their off-grid infrastructure, particularly if their site has access to a stream or other water source. Hydropower is a viable solution for off-grid populations looking for a reliable and renewable energy source because of its output consistency and dependability.

An alternate energy source called geothermal power uses the heat naturally present in the Earth. This type of energy uses the natural temperature differential between the Earth's surface and its depths. Geothermal systems usually use steam or hot water to power turbines that produce energy. For off-grid living, these systems provide a reliable and environmentally friendly source of electricity, particularly in regions with geothermal potential. Because of its reputation for dependability and low environmental impact, geothermal power is a desirable substitute for people looking for environmentally friendly energy options.

The most well-known alternative energy source is solar power, which uses sunshine to create electricity. Solar panels, called photovoltaic (PV) cells, directly convert sunlight into electrical energy. Off-grid homesteaders widely use solar panels to provide electricity for appliances, lights, household necessities, and other uses. Because solar power systems are scalable and modular, homesteaders can tailor their installations to suit their needs for energy and available space. Due to its adaptability and potential for off-grid and decentralized uses, solar power has become increasingly popular in the quest for energy independence.

Another powerful alternative power source is wind energy, produced by the kinetic energy of flowing air. Using a generator, wind turbines transform the spinning action of their turbine blades into electrical energy. Small-scale wind turbines are frequently used in off-grid places with regular wind patterns to supplement other energy sources. Wind energy is incredibly appealing because of its adaptability and ability to generate electricity day and night. Even with issues like fluctuating wind speeds and possible aesthetic effects, technological developments are improving the efficiency and suitability of wind power for off-grid living.

Revolutionary technology has made Emerging alternative power sources possible in recent years. For example, tidal and wave energy uses the energy of the ocean's tides and waves to create electricity. Wave energy systems use the kinetic energy of waves, whereas tidal energy systems exploit the rise and fall of the tides to drive turbines. Despite their early phases of development, these technologies show promise as sustainable alternatives, particularly for coastal towns hoping to use the ocean's energy for off-grid electricity.

Because many renewable energy sources are intermittent, energy storage is essential to increasing the efficiency of alternative power sources. Lithium-ion and lead-acid batteries, for example, allow surplus energy produced during peak hours to be stored for later use. When renewable energy production is minimal, like on cloudy days or during calm winds, energy storage systems give off-grid homesteaders a dependable power source. As battery costs have come down and technology has advanced, energy storage has become essential to building a reliable, stable off-grid power system.

The benefits of alternative power sources are not limited to environmental aspects; they also encompass economic and social aspects. Many alternative energy systems are decentralized, allowing communities and people to take charge of their energy generation. Off-grid living fosters greater independence from centralized utility networks by integrating alternate power sources smoothly, emphasizing self-sufficiency. Additionally, alternative energy technology can boost regional economies by generating installation, maintenance, and manufacturing jobs.

Potential cost savings highlight the economic benefits of alternate power sources even more. Even while some alternative energy systems need a significant initial investment, they frequently have lower ongoing operating costs than conventional utility-based electricity. State and municipal governments commonly provide incentives, refunds, and tax credits to promote alternative energy sources, making the shift more affordable for people who want to live energy-independent lives. A global transition toward a more sustainable and decentralized energy paradigm has been sparked by alternative power sources' economic viability and environmental benefits.

There are issues with alternative energy sources that must be carefully thought out and planned for. The unpredictability of many renewable resources, like wind and sunshine, is a prevalent problem. The consistency of energy output can be affected by cloudy days, nights, or low wind times. This calls for incorporating energy storage technologies or hybrid systems that mix numerous sources. It takes careful system design and optimization to balance the intermittent character of various renewable energy sources and the dependability of the power supply.

Land use and environmental effects are important factors to consider, especially for larger-scale alternative energy projects. Large tracts of land may be needed for wind turbines, solar farms, and other infrastructures, which could affect biodiversity and ecosystems. Careful site selection, environmental impact assessments, and community involvement are necessary to minimize negative consequences and guarantee that alternative energy initiatives comply with ecological stewardship and sustainability standards.

Resource extraction, manufacture, and disposal effects on the environment present difficulties for energy storage technology. The business needs to handle issues related to the extraction of resources like lithium, cobalt, and nickel, which can have social and ecological repercussions as demand for batteries rises. Minimizing the environmental impact of energy storage technologies will also require developing sustainable production techniques and effective recycling procedures.

CHAPTER V

Water Harvesting and Management

Rainwater Collection

Modern rainwater collection is an innovative and sustainable water management technique, reviving an ancient practice. This approach captures and stores rainwater for irrigation, landscape upkeep, toilet flushing, and drinking. Rainwater collection is essential for water security in off-grid life, where self-sufficiency and resource conservation are paramount. This section examines the principles, applications, benefits, drawbacks, and transforming effects of rainwater collection on off-grid populations seeking a more sustainable and resilient lifestyle.

Rainwater collecting captures raindrops on roofs,

gutters, and other catchments. The collected rainwater is piped and filtered into storage tanks for later use. Rainwater collection systems are ideal for off-grid living due to their ease and versatility. Rainwater collection can lessen dependence on external sources and provide a locally regulated, sustainable water source for off-grid homesteaders.

Rainwater collecting in off-grid living meets many water

demands without centralized water infrastructure. It is mainly used for irrigation, supporting gardens, crops, and beautification. Rainwater, without additions like city water, is suitable for plants. Rainwater can also water livestock on the homestead, making it self-sufficient. Rainwater may flush toilets, wash clothing, and even drink when adequately treated and filtered.

Rainwater collection has many benefits, making it a sustainable water management option. Water conservation is a significant benefit. Homesteaders minimize water demand on local water sources by capturing rainwater that would otherwise run off or be lost, protecting ecosystems and water cycles. This conservation-minded strategy fits with off-grid living's emphasis on minimizing environmental effects and harmonizing with nature.

Rainwater collection systems are easy to build and maintain, giving off-grid homesteaders a cheap and accessible water supply. The most straightforward rainwater harvesting system includes collection surfaces (usually rooftops), gutters, downspouts, filters, and storage tanks. Individuals or communities installing a rainwater collection system can easily find and install these components. Rainwater harvesting is decentralized so homesteaders can scale it to their requirements and space.

Stormwater management is a significant environmental benefit of rainwater collection. Stormwater runoff in conventional urban areas can cause erosion, floods, and polluting waterways. Capturing and storing rainfall reduces runoff and its influence on the landscape. Rainwater collection helps off-grid homesteaders manage water, use land responsibly, and reduce environmental impact.

When properly collected and kept, rainfall is typically better than conventional water. Rainwater is gentle and free of minerals and additives in groundwater and municipal water. Its lack of mineral deposits makes it ideal for irrigation systems requiring high water quality. Rain can provide off-grid homesteaders with a reliable and locally derived drinking water source if treated and filtered.

The economic benefits of rainwater collection make it appealing for off-grid living. Homesteaders can avoid costly water services and well drilling by capturing rainwater for multiple applications. Rainwater harvesting systems are a cost-effective long-term water supply solution due to low operational and maintenance costs. Rainwater collection is practical and cost-effective in areas with limited access to water.

Despite its many benefits, rainwater collecting offers hurdles that off-grid homesteaders must overcome to maintain system efficacy and safety. Rainfall frequency and intensity vary, presenting a difficulty. Water scarcity may result from sporadic or unpredictable rainfall, depending on location. Homesteaders in such areas must plan and size their rainwater collection systems to accommodate rainfall variability, possibly using larger storage tanks or additional water sources.

Safe and effective rainwater use requires quality maintenance. Rainwater can pick up pollutants from rooftops or the air during its descent. Bird droppings, dust, pollen, and industrial contaminants may enter rainfall. Homesteaders use mesh filters and first flush diverters to remove dirt and impurities before water enters storage tanks. Rainwater quality must be maintained by cleaning gutters and examining the system for problems.

Microbial contamination is another concern, especially if the rainwater is for drinking. Rainwater is suitable for irrigation and non-potable uses, although it may need filtration, UV sterilization, or chlorination before consumption. To protect rainwater drinkers, off-grid homesteaders must evaluate and treat water quality.

The local climate, water demand, and catchment area must be considered while designing and sizing rainwater collection systems. Oversizing or undersizing the system wastes resources on storage capacity or fails to meet water demand during dry periods. Rainwater harvesting systems must be carefully planned in off-grid living situations, considering historical rainfall data and water usage patterns.

Finally, rainwater collection provides off-grid homesteaders with locally managed, adaptable, and eco-friendly water. It can be used for irrigation, domestic usage, and drinking water with sufficient treatment. Rainwater collecting is integral to off-grid living due to its water conservation, ease of installation, environmental benefits, and economic savings. Despite rainfall variability, water quality maintenance, and system design, rainwater collection systems empower individuals and communities to control their water supply, making off-grid living more resilient and sustainable. Rainwater represents self-sufficiency and environmental responsibility, helping off-grid homesteaders achieve a more sustainable and water-secure future.

Well Systems

An enduring technique for reaching groundwater, well systems have been essential to providing dependable and independent water supplies for societies worldwide. As one of the central tenets of off-grid living is independence from centralized utilities, well systems are essential to ensuring a locally managed and sustainable water supply. This section explores the complexities of sound systems, including their fundamental ideas, uses, benefits, drawbacks, and potential transformational effects for off-grid communities aiming for a more resilient and water-secure way of life.

Drawing water from subterranean groundwater reservoirs is the basic idea behind well systems. The purpose of wells is to transport water to the surface for domestic purposes, drinking, and irrigation. Well, systems are a standard primary or supplemental water supply for off-grid homesteaders, particularly in areas with restricted access to surface water or municipal utilities. The System's adaptability and independence fit well with the off-grid lifestyle's emphasis on self-sufficiency and resilience in achieving fundamental necessities.

A steady and dependable drinking water supply is one of the primary uses for sound systems. Groundwater, found in aquifers beneath the surface of the Earth, is frequently protected from pollution and contamination that could harm surface water supplies. These underground reservoirs provide pure, naturally filtered water for consumption, which is achieved through wells. When living off the grid, when drinking water quality and safety are critical, well systems give a stable, locally managed option to depend on outside water suppliers.

Well, systems are helpful for more than just providing clean drinking water; they may be used for various home and agricultural purposes. A common practice among homesteaders is watering gardens, crops, and cattle with healthy water. This application is critical in off-grid living situations, where access to water is essential for maintaining crops to extract water from wells gives people and communities the ability to produce food sustainably, which lessens reliance on outside food sources and increases the all-around resilience of off-grid living.

Systems have several benefits, so off-grid regions are adopting them in large numbers. One of their main advantages is their autonomy, which enables homesteaders to monitor and control their water supply independently of centralized utilities. Off-grid life is made possible by sound systems, which relieve people of their need for municipal water supplies and their need to connect to vast, frequently remote water distribution networks. The spirit of off-grid living is defined by this independence, which is consistent with the values of environmental responsibility and self-sufficiency.

Another significant benefit of sound systems is their dependability, particularly advantageous in areas with plentiful and naturally replenished groundwater. Wells draw water from aquifers that are resilient to changes in weather, offering a steady water supply even in dry spells. Because of its consistency, off-grid societies are more resilient and have an endless water supply for necessities. Furthermore, homesteaders can modify their well's capacity to satisfy fluctuating water demands because healthy systems are decentralized and scalable.

Well, systems have significant environmental benefits, especially when compared to surface water sources. Because layers of rock and soil protect it, groundwater is frequently less vulnerable to contamination by pollutants, pesticides, or diseases than surface water. By lessening the ecological effect of human activity on nearby water bodies, well systems preserve the quality of water resources. Off-grid homesteaders actively contribute to groundwater conservation and protection by managing their wells responsibly, which builds a long-lasting bond with the environment.

One reason why well systems are popular for off-grid living is their simplicity. Drilling or excavating a hole into the ground until the water table, or the point at which the ground is saturated with water, is reached is the fundamental method of building a well. Next, a pump is fitted to raise the water level in the well, and a casing is added to avoid contamination and collapse. Even though more sophisticated drilling methods and sound technology are available, off-grid homesteaders with different degrees of skill can still construct traditional wells due to their ease of use.

Water has a constant, naturally cool temperature, which is an added benefit for off-grid living. This quality can be beneficial for some farming methods, such as fish farming or aquaculture, where the health of aquatic animals depends on temperature stability. Off-grid homesteaders can maximize their agricultural and aquacultural pursuits by taking advantage of the natural temperature properties of healthy water, thus improving the overall sustainability of their lifestyle.

Off-grid homesteaders must overcome several obstacles with sound systems, notwithstanding their benefits, to guarantee their water supply's efficiency and security. The risk of over-extraction or groundwater resource depletion is one major obstacle. The water table may drop, and less water may be available if wells extract water from aquifers more quickly than they can replenish naturally. Reducing the risk of over-extraction requires using sustainable, healthy management techniques, such as tracking water levels, figuring out acceptable withdrawal rates, and putting conservation measures in place.

Since many factors can affect groundwater quality, contamination is an ongoing worry with sound systems. The integrity of healthy water can be jeopardized by poor sturdy construction, inadequate casing maintenance, or proximity to sources of pollution. Homesteaders need to take precautions against contaminants getting into the well and be on the lookout for any sources of contamination. It is essential to regularly test well water for impurities like bacteria, nitrates, or heavy metals to make sure it is safe to drink.

In off-grid living situations, the energy needs of healthy systems, especially those that depend on pumps, might provide difficulties. Off-grid homesteaders must look into alternate power sources, including solar or wind energy, to power their well pumps because traditional well pumps might need electricity. To ensure sustainable operation, the right pump system must be chosen, considering energy efficiency and dependability. of healthy systems in remote locations. Regular upkeep and sporadic repairs are also required to maintain the pump and related machinery in top working order.

The geological features of the surrounding area significantly influence the viability and efficiency of sound systems. Geological formations in some areas may make healthy drilling difficult or prohibitively expensive. To establish whether digging a well is appropriate, off-grid homesteaders must perform extensive geological evaluations that include measurements of the water table's depth and soil composition. Geological research aids in making well- informed decisions and assisting homesteaders in selecting the most practical water supply and well- system configuration for their particular site.

Local laws and permitting procedures may also impact installing and operating sound systems in off-grid living. Groundwater management, water rights, and healthy buildings are subject to particular regulations in some areas. To ensure compliance and prudent water use, homesteaders must become informed about local laws, secure the required licenses, and follow best practices. By interacting with communities and local government agencies, it is possible to promote a cooperative approach to deploying healthy systems, cultivate goodwill, and resolve potential issues.

Water Conservation

A vital part of sustainable living, water conservation has grown more critical in light of the world's expanding water crises. Protecting and effectively managing water resources is more critical than ever due to changing climate patterns, growing populations, and stressed ecosystems. In the world of off-grid life, when environmental care and self-sufficiency are essential principles, water-saving techniques become necessary. In the context of off-grid living, this section examines water conservation's fundamentals, tactics, benefits, drawbacks, and revolutionary effects, highlighting its significance in promoting a robust and sustainable way of life.

Fundamentally, water conservation is about using water resources wisely and effectively to reduce waste and maintain a sustainable balance between ecological health and human needs. Homesteaders living off the grid, who frequently inhabit regions with restricted access to centralized water facilities, understand the intrinsic worth of water as a limited and valuable resource. Adopting water-saving techniques becomes a matter of convenience and a core morality consistent with off-grid living concepts.

Optimizing the efficiency of water use in all areas of everyday life is one of the fundamental tenets of water conservation. This improvement applies to both indoor and outdoor water usage in off-grid residences. Low-flow plumbing equipment, like showerheads, toilets, and faucets, is essential for reducing indoor water use. Water efficiency in outdoor gardening can be enhanced via rainwater collection devices, greywater reuse, and intelligent planting techniques. When taken as a whole, these steps guarantee that every drop of water is used efficiently and reduces needless waste.

Rainwater collection devices are a mainstay of water-saving strategies for off-grid homesteaders. By collecting and storing rainwater for later use, this technique helps to lessen reliance on outside water sources. Rainwater is naturally collected on rooftops and directed into storage tanks. After it has been appropriately treated, the collected rainwater can be used for various things, such as irrigation, livestock watering, and even home needs. By supplying a locally managed water supply, rainwater collection improves resilience while simultaneously conserving water.

Another critical tactic in the off-grid water-saving toolbox is graywater reuse. Water that has been used sparingly for tasks like laundry, dishwashing, and bathing is known as water. Off-grid homesteaders redirect greywater to secondary uses rather than sending all household water into sewage facilities. Graywater may be sent this way to irrigate landscape areas or gardens, completing a closed-loop system that reuses water on the farm. Reusing greywater reduces the environmental effect of treating and releasing wastewater while conserving water.

Water-efficient landscaping techniques are based on off-grid living concepts. Homesteaders prioritize water conservation through xeriscaping, use mulching to keep soil moisture, and select drought-tolerant plants. Off-grid homeowners develop outdoor spaces that thrive with little water input by matching their landscaping selections to the local climate and surroundings. These thoughtful landscaping techniques support a healthy coexistence of human habitation and the local ecosystem while also helping to conserve water.

Water conservation in off-grid life has benefits beyond the immediate preservation of water supplies. One crucial advantage is the decrease in energy used for water distribution and purification. In conventional centralized water supply systems, a significant amount of energy is used in the long-distance pumping, treating, and transporting water. Off-grid homesteaders reduce the need for centralized water infrastructure by conserving water locally, which lowers their environmental impact and saves energy.

Economic factors further highlight the benefits of conserving water when living off the grid. For their electrical demands, many off-grid homesteads rely on renewable energy sources like solar or wind power—lower energy needs for pumping and processing water result from conserving water and lowering costs. Furthermore, off-grid homesteaders can gain financially from well-designed rainwater collection and greywater reuse systems since they reduce the need to drill new wells or invest in elaborate water infrastructure.

Water conservation and the more general objectives of environmental sustainability work hand in hand. Off-grid living lessens the strain on nearby ecosystems and water bodies by using less water. Conscientious water conservation methods are beneficial for aquatic environments, which are frequently susceptible to variations in water availability. Preserving natural water sources upholds the values of environmental stewardship essential to off-grid living and promotes a harmonious coexistence between human populations and the environment.

Water conservation in off-grid life has many benefits but drawbacks that call for careful planning and community involvement. Water availability variation is an issue, particularly in areas vulnerable to drought or seasonal water scarcity. Off-grid homesteaders must carefully evaluate their local climate, water supplies, and usage patterns to create water-saving plans that work with the environment's natural cycles. To navigate shifting situations, water management strategies must be flexible and adaptable.

Though it empowers people and communities, off-grid living's decentralized structure makes it difficult to carry out extensive water conservation programs. Off-grid homesteads are autonomous, unlike centralized water utilities that can impose conservation requirements on a large customer base. Communal collaboration and group efforts become crucial to effective water conservation when living off the grid. To get the most out of their efforts, homesteaders can organize neighborhood water committees, exchange best practices, and work together to implement water-saving devices.

Off-grid water conservation also takes into account the requirement for efficient water treatment. Although beneficial, systems for collecting rainwater and reusing graywater must be adequately filtered and treated to guarantee the quality of the water. Off-grid homesteaders must invest in appropriate water treatment technologies, like UV sterilization, chemical disinfection, or filtration, to ensure that the water used again on the property satisfies safety and health regulations. Water conservation must be balanced with the need to supply safe and drinkable water, which calls for an all-encompassing strategy that considers quality and quantity.

In off-grid communities, awareness-building and education are essential for overcoming obstacles and promoting a water-saving culture. Homesteaders can participate in outreach programs, workshops, and knowledge-sharing initiatives to encourage water-conscious practices because they are frequently closely connected to the natural environment. Developing a sustainable water culture in off-grid communities requires instilling a sense of responsibility and educating people about the connection between water conservation and general well-being.

Pursuing robust and sustainable off-grid living is contingent upon water conservation. Off-grid homesteaders embrace water conservation as a guiding concept and achieve it through rainwater gathering, greywater reuse, efficient water fixtures, and thoughtful landscaping techniques. The benefits, which include reduced energy use, financial gains, and environmental responsibility, highlight how water conservation has a revolutionary effect on off-grid living. Overcoming obstacles like fluctuating water availability and the requirement for efficient water treatment calls for careful planning, community cooperation, and continual.

CHAPTER VI

Sustainable Agriculture Practices

Organic Farming Techniques

Based on sustainability, environmental stewardship, and holistic agricultural practices, organic farming methods are growing in popularity as a practical and moral method of producing food. Growing crops using organic farming methods is essential for making wholesome and eco-friendly foods when living off the grid, where sustainability and reducing environmental damage are critical. This section examines the fundamental ideas, practices, advantages, difficulties, and revolutionary effects of organic farming methods in the context of off- grid agriculture, focusing on how they promote resilient and sustainable food systems.

An emphasis on soil fertility and health is fundamental to organic farming. Using techniques like crop rotation, cover crops, and composting, organic farmers prioritize creating and preserving nutrient-rich soils. By breaking down organic materials like leftover food and plant waste, composting creates nutrient-rich humus that improves soil fertility and structure. The deliberate planting of particular crops between main crops to protect and cover the soil, reduce erosion, increase organic matter, and fix nitrogen is known as cover cropping. Crop rotation, which involves planting a succession of crops, maintains soil fertility while disrupting pest and disease cycles. These methods help maintain soil health, which is essential to sustainable farming practices.

Organic farming is distinguished by its avoidance of synthetic chemical inputs. Organic farmers use natural solutions to control pests and improve soil fertility rather than relying on traditional fertilizers and pesticides. To manage pests and lessen the need for chemical interventions, beneficial insects, crop rotation, and companion planting are used. In addition, compost, manure, and green manure cover crops are examples of fertilizers permitted for use by organic farmers and frequently used to supply crops with vital nutrients. Organic farming helps preserve biodiversity, reduce pollution to the environment, and improve the general health of ecosystems by avoiding synthetic chemicals.

Organic farming strongly emphasizes biodiversity, and techniques like agroforestry and polyculture help build resilient and varied ecosystems. Polyculture entails cultivating many crops in the exact location to replicate natural ecosystems and lower the chance of crop failure from pests or diseases. Agroforestry incorporates shrubs and trees into agricultural landscapes to promote biodiversity and offer extra advantages, including windbreaks, shade, and homes for beneficial creatures. A more resilient and flexible agricultural system is encouraged, natural pest control is enabled, and including various plant species improves the overall ecological balance.

Organic agricultural practices are in perfect harmony with the concepts of self-sufficiency in off-grid environments, where relying on outside inputs may not be feasible. Getting and transporting synthetic insecticides and fertilizers might take much work for off-grid homesteaders. Organic farming enables people to grow food without outside chemicals by providing a decentralized and locally adaptive strategy. Off-grid living's resource-efficient philosophy is reflected in the closed-loop nature of biological systems, where waste products become inputs for the following cycle.

Organic farming techniques strongly emphasize soil protection, which addresses the erosion and degradation frequently linked to conventional agricultural practices. Organic farmers improve soil structure and reduce soil erosion using techniques like contour plowing, cover crops, and agroforestry. To lessen soil erosion and water flow on slopes, contour plowing entails plows following the land's natural contours. In addition to improving soil structure and halting nutrient loss, cover crops shield exposed soil from erosion. Furthermore, agroforestry systems with carefully placed trees and bushes aid in soil stabilization, erosion prevention, and the creation of microclimates favorable to plant growth.

Many organic farming methods include water conservation as a fundamental component, illustrating the relationship between agriculture and the broader ecosystem. Water conservation and soil moisture retention are achieved through mulching and effective irrigation systems. Mulching is covering the soil surrounding plants with organic materials, such as leaves or straw, to create a barrier that keeps moisture in the soil, inhibits weed growth, and controls soil temperature. Organic farms generally give rainwater gathering techniques priority to collect and store precipitation for use in irrigation during periods of drought. An off-grid lifestyle, where prudent water resource management is essential to self-sufficiency, is consistent with the emphasis on water conservation.

A key element of organic farming is crop diversity and seed sovereignty, which promote resilience in shifting environmental conditions. Since they maintain their genetic diversity and flexibility throughout time, open-pollinated and heirloom varieties are given preference by organic farmers. In contrast, monocultures and hybrid types are prevalent in industrial agriculture. Seed saving and exchange become essential in off-grid living since access to outside seeds and inputs may be limited. Off-grid agriculture is made more resilient by using organic farming techniques, which help preserve traditional and locally adapted crop varieties.

Producing healthful and nutritious food is just one of the advantages of organic farming and its positive effects on the environment. Due to their lack of synthetic fertilizers and pesticides, organic crops frequently have higher concentrations of healthy substances like micronutrients and antioxidants. Research has indicated that fruits and vegetables that are grown organically may have higher levels of specific vitamins and minerals. Furthermore, cattle welfare is given top priority in organic farming practices, which emphasize natural diets, access to pasture, and humane treatment. The nutritional value and health advantages of organic farming enhance the general well-being of off-grid communities, where dependence on regional food supply is essential.

An essential component of organic farming is economic sustainability, especially in off-grid environments with few financial resources. Organic agriculture offers long-term economic viability, even though the initial shift to organic practices can need modifications. Organic farmers frequently see cost benefits over time by decreasing reliance on outside inputs and mitigating the effects of pricey, synthetic inputs. Furthermore, organic farmers in off-grid environments can establish direct contact with consumers, strengthening economic resilience and promoting community, thanks to the focus on local and direct marketing channels like farmers' markets and community-supported agriculture (CSA).

Off-grid organic farming has many benefits, but drawbacks also need to be carefully considered and accommodated. Managing diseases and pests without artificial pesticides can be difficult and necessitate a thorough grasp of ecological principles and alternative tactics. Organic farmers can reduce pest pressures by utilizing companion planting, beneficial insects, and integrated pest management (IPM) strategies. Nonetheless, obtaining efficient pest management without depending on traditional pesticides necessitates a careful and wise approach.

Off-grid homesteaders frequently face a learning curve

while switching to organic agricultural methods, which requires knowledge and skill development. It takes expertise and experience to fully comprehend the nuances of crop rotations, soil health, and natural pest control techniques. Gaining proficiency in organic farming may call for commitment to lifelong learning and dedication in off-grid living, where people frequently wear many roles. Off-grid homesteaders' ability to grow their food sustainably can be improved by providing them with educational materials, workshops, and community assistance as they embrace organic farming methods.

Certification and market access present obstacles for

off-grid organic farmers who want to sell their goods outside of their immediate community. Off-grid homesteads may need help complying with the documentation requirements of organic certification, even if they offer a recognized standard for organic products.

Fees as well as inspections. Furthermore, access to

mainstream markets may be restricted in specific off-grid locales due to their geographic remoteness. To overcome these obstacles and establish direct customer relationships, off-grid homesteaders should investigate alternate marketing techniques such as neighborhood farmers' markets, farm-to-table programs, and community-supported agriculture.

Permaculture Principles

The word "permaculture," first used in the 1970s by Bill Mollison and David Holmgren, refers to a comprehensive and regenerative method of planning human communities to resemble natural ecosystems. Permaculture, rooted in sustainability, adaptability, and collaboration with the natural world, has developed into a framework that serves as a roadmap for people and groups who want to live more peacefully and independently. Permaculture principles provide a lighthouse for building resilient and regenerative systems in the context of off-grid life, where the pursuit of sustainability and low environmental effects is vital. In the context of off-grid life, this section examines permaculture's core ideas and its uses, advantages, difficulties, and transformative power.

The fundamental tenet of permaculture is "observe and interact," which highlights how crucial it is to comprehend a site's natural patterns and processes before creating interventions. This idea of off-grid living necessitates a close relationship with the local ecosystem, which includes the climate, topography, water flows, and biodiversity. Off-grid homesteaders learn about the unique qualities of their land via close observation, which empowers them to make well-informed choices about resource management, sustainable design, and the production of food and other resources.

"Catch and store energy," which promotes the effective use of natural energies, is another fundamental permaculture concept. Off-grid homesteads frequently incorporate renewable energy sources like solar and wind turbines to suit their electricity needs. Furthermore, permaculture strongly emphasizes gathering and storing water through methods like earthworks and rainwater collection. These tactics fit right in with the off-grid lifestyle philosophy, which emphasizes the importance of using renewable and local energy sources to become self-sufficient.

The "obtain a yield" idea emphasizes the importance of designing systems that provide observable and advantageous results. This could entail planning food forests in off-grid permaculture, where various perennial and edible plants are grown for a steady harvest. Including multipurpose features is a great way to maximize the return from each component in the design. One example is fruit trees, which serve as shade and food sources. Off-grid homesteaders increase their ability to live sustainably and independently by prioritizing systems that yield observable results.

The permaculture principle "Apply self-regulation and accept feedback" highlights the significance of preserving systemic balance and drawing lessons from intervention results. When it comes to off-grid life, this idea emphasizes resilience and adaptation. Homesteaders living off the grid must constantly evaluate and modify their systems in reaction to shifting weather patterns, input from the land, and changing community requirements. Off-grid systems must be able to accept feedback and self-regulate to continue being responsive, dynamic, and in balance with the environment.

Additionally, permaculture promotes the idea of "use and value renewable resources and services," which pushes off-grid homesteaders to prioritize regenerative and sustainable methods. This could include using companion planting to reduce pests, using animals to manage weeds and improve soil fertility, or leveraging the natural fertilizing powers of nitrogen-fixing plants. The restoration and regeneration of the land they live on is facilitated by off-grid permaculturists who respect ecological services and renewable resources.

The permaculture concept of "produce no waste" promotes resource efficiency and recycling. This idea is consistent with the off-grid lifestyle's goal of minimizing environmental effects and creating a closed-loop system. Off-grid homesteaders use composting, mulching, and recycling techniques to turn organic waste into a valuable resource for soil fertility rather than a pollution source. The idea is to establish a regenerative cycle that embodies the permaculture principle of cradle-to-cradle, where waste from one element becomes a resource for another.

Off-grid homesteaders are encouraged to identify and use natural patterns and structures in their design processes by following the "design from patterns to details" philosophy. Homesteaders can construct designs that blend with the surrounding terrain by understanding the broader climate patterns, water flows, and ecosystem dynamics. This strategy encourages human activity and the environment to work harmoniously and integratively. This idea directs the development of robust and functional designs that capture the innate intelligence of off-grid permaculture systems.

The permaculture principle "integrate rather than segregate" emphasizes how parts within a design are interrelated. Homesteaders living off the grid put this idea into practice by developing various interdependent systems. For instance, water collection systems can be placed close to regions with high water demand or incorporate plants that draw helpful insects near crops. This idea encourages the growth of ecosystems in which every component supports and improves the system's overall functionality.

The idea of "use small and slow solutions," which promotes incremental and context-appropriate interventions, is encouraged by permaculture. This idea encourages a systematic and careful approach to system development when living off the grid. Off-grid homesteaders carry out small-scale experiments, monitor the outcomes, and make necessary adjustments rather than enforcing abrupt and drastic changes. This method enables a more precise alignment with natural processes and a more detailed understanding of the land.

"is a permaculture tenet that honors the sturdiness and adaptability that result from ecosystem diversity. This idea is embraced by off-grid homesteads, which shun monoculture techniques, encourage genetic diversity, and cultivate various plant and animal species. Diversity supports sustainable off-grid living and permaculture ideals by increasing resistance to pests and diseases, enhancing ecosystem stability, and offering a wide range of harvests.

A further tenet of permaculture is to "use edges and value the marginal." Transitional zones and edges are essential components of designs that off-grid homesteaders understand. These intersections of various elements or ecosystems are frequently rich in biodiversity and have the potential to be fruitful locations. Off-grid permaculturists optimize the usefulness and diversity of their systems by planning with edges in mind, for instance, adding vegetation that does well in transitional areas or developing varied edge habitats home to various species.

The idea of "creatively use and respond to change" recognizes that change is inevitable and invites off-grid homesteaders to seize the chance it presents for creativity and adaptation. Off-grid permaculturists are always open to new ideas and adaptable methods, whether in response to changing climatic patterns, community requirements, or input from the earth. This idea highlights how dynamic and ever-changing off-grid living is and how long-term resilience depends on one's capacity to adjust to change.

Off-grid life incorporates larger community and social aspects and individual homesteads, all based on applying permaculture principles. Through the promotion of communal bonds, information exchange, and cooperative endeavors, off-grid permaculturists aid in the development of robust and interwoven networks. Shared resource management, collaborative projects, and community-supported agriculture are examples of how permaculture concepts can be expanded to handle group issues and improve the general sustainability of off-grid communities.

Although permaculture concepts provide a thorough and all-encompassing framework for sustainable living, there are obstacles to their successful implementation in off-grid situations. The absence of outside resources, knowledge, and technological know-how can provide challenges for off-grid homesteaders looking to implement permaculture plans. Furthermore, to successfully incorporate permaculture concepts into their off-grid lifestyle, people may need to acquire a wide range of skills, from agroecology to renewable energy systems, due to the necessity for self-reliance.

Integrating Livestock

Including cattle in off-grid living systems is a complex strategy beyond conventional farming. Livestock, including pigs, cows, goats, and chickens, can be significant to an off-grid homesteading operation since they improve soil fertility, food production, waste management, and general resilience. In examining the fundamentals, strategies, advantages, difficulties, and revolutionary effects of incorporating livestock into off- grid living, this section highlights the cooperative connections that may be established between people, animals, and the environment.

The fundamental idea behind incorporating livestock into off-grid life is symbiosis, the coexistence of humans and animals in mutually beneficial partnerships. For example, chickens are excellent at controlling pests because they scavenge for insects and weed seeds, which lessens the need for chemical treatments. They contribute to the household's food security by giving a consistent supply of meat and eggs in exchange. Similarly, cows and goats contribute to the quality of pastures, inhibit the growth of exotic plants, and provide milk for dairy products through controlled rotational grazing.

Livestock and off-grid living are intertwined to promote a regenerative cycle in which the animals' presence increases the homestead's resilience and output.

The fact that animals contribute to sustainable food production is one of the main advantages of incorporating them into off-grid life. Besides their ability to repel pests, chickens also offer a reliable supply of meat and eggs. When kept under control, goats and cows provide milk, cheese, and meat. Because they are omnivores, pigs can convert organic waste and food scraps into premium pork. Off-grid homesteaders increase their self-sufficiency, lessen their reliance on outside food sources, and promote a closed-loop system where waste from one element becomes a resource for another by integrating livestock into their food sources.

In off-grid living systems, livestock is essential to land management and soil fertility. Homesteaders can replicate natural grazing patterns and reduce overgrazing using rotational grazing, which involves moving animals systematically between different pasture sites. This method keeps pastures healthy and improves soil structure, stimulates the cycling of nutrients, and fosters the development of various plant species. Livestock manure replenishes soil nutrients and adds to the homestead's general fertility, making it an excellent organic fertilizer. Livestock integration thus becomes a crucial component of regenerative agriculture, promoting robust food production and healthy ecosystems.

Another area of off-grid living where livestock integration works well is waste management. Because of their insatiable thirst for leftover food and garden debris, chickens aid in composting, which turns organic material into fertilizer that is high in nutrients.

Pigs are well known for eating a variety of food scraps, and their dung can be composted to provide beneficial soil nutrients. Livestock and trash management work together to support the off-grid lifestyle tenets of resource efficiency and environmental sustainability.

Moreover, incorporating livestock into off-grid systems fosters the creation of diverse and comprehensive landscapes. This strategy is best illustrated by the practice of agroforestry, which mixes the cultivation of trees with livestock and crops. In addition to providing shelter, shade, and windbreaks, trees also serve as food for some animals. In turn, livestock helps control vegetation and improve soil fertility, resulting in a well- balanced integration of various landscape aspects. As a result, a robust and multipurpose setting that adheres to sustainable off-grid living and permaculture principles is created.

Nevertheless, integrating cattle into off-grid systems has its challenges. One major worry is the requirement for adequate land and good management techniques to prevent overgrazing and land degradation. Careful monitoring of stocking rates and rotational grazing becomes crucial in off-grid living situations where land may be scarce. Overgrazing can jeopardize the ecosystem's general health since it can cause pastureland degradation, biodiversity loss, and soil erosion.

Another area for improvement is managing water, especially in dry or semi-arid off-grid regions. Off-grid homesteaders must install effective water systems to guarantee a sustained supply of clean water for their livestock, which need access to it. Ponds, well-maintained water sources, and rainwater collection are essential to successful livestock integration. Water shortage presents issues for off-grid livestock management. Still, conservation measures like building water-efficient troughs and rotating grazing by natural water cycles can help lessen such challenges.

An essential factor in incorporating cattle into off-grid living is animal care. Responsible livestock management requires humane slaughter procedures, appropriate nutrition, access to suitable housing, and ethical treatment of animals. Off-grid homesteaders need to put their animals' welfare first because they understand that treating livestock ethically is not only morally required but also crucial to integrated systems' long-term viability and success.

An essential factor in the effectiveness of off-grid integration is the chosen cattle species. Animals differ in their needs, personalities, and ecological effects. For example, goats are renowned for their browsing behaviors and landscape adaptation, which makes them appropriate for rugged terrain. Conversely, hens are adaptable hunters with a negligible environmental impact. The off-grid homestead's objectives and ecological conditions must be considered while choosing livestock species to ensure a harmonic integration that optimizes advantages and minimizes potential disadvantages.

Homesteaders living off the grid must also consider the zoning and regulatory implications of integrating animals. Certain kinds and quantities of animals may be restricted by local laws, especially in rural areas. Setback distances, housing requirements, and waste management techniques may all be governed by zoning rules. Maintaining good ties with the neighborhood and staying out of trouble with the law depends on following these rules.

Adding livestock to off-grid living systems provides a comprehensive and regenerative strategy for long-term sustainable homesteading. Responsible livestock integration has revolutionary effects that range from improved soil fertility and diverse food production to effective waste management and comprehensive landscape planning. Problems like water scarcity, land management, animal welfare, and regulatory compliance demand careful planning and well-considered solutions. Off-grid homesteaders help to create robust and peaceful living systems where people, animals, and the environment cohabit in symbiotic partnerships as they overcome these obstacles. Livestock plays an essential role in the complex dance of integrated living, serving as partners in the quest for ecological balance and self-sufficiency as well as a food source.

CHAPTER VII

Food Preservation and Storage

Canning and Fermentation

Traditional food preservation techniques like canning and fermenting have gained new significance when considering off-grid life. These time-tested methods provide effective and long-lasting solutions for off-grid homesteaders who aim to decrease waste, increase the amount of produce grown on their property, and lessen their reliance on outside food sources. In the context of off-grid living, this section explores the fundamentals, procedures, advantages, difficulties, and transformative power of canning and fermentation. It emphasizes the significance of these practices in maintaining food security, extending the harvest, and encouraging a connection to the seasonal rhythms of homestead life.

Food is preserved by canning, a practice that dates back to the early 1800s, which includes sealing food in jars and heating them to kill bacteria that cause deterioration. This method creates a vacuum seal that keeps air from entering and stops bacteria, yeasts, and mold from growing. Preserving fruits, vegetables, jams, sauces, and even meats is excellent for canning. Canning offers a dependable way to extend the shelf life of perishable goods in off-grid living situations where access to refrigeration may be limited. This allows homesteaders to enjoy the fullness of the crop all year long.

While pressure canning is utilized for low-acid items like meats and vegetables, water bath canning is typically used for high-acid goods like fruits and pickles. While pressure canning uses steam pressure to reach higher temperatures and reduce the danger of botulism, water bath canning involves immersing sealed jars in boiling water. Both techniques require careful consideration of cleanliness, exact timing, and adherence to safety regulations to guarantee food preservation without sacrificing its quality.

Contrarily, fermentation is a natural process that turns sugars and starches into acids, gasses, and alcohol using microorganisms, primarily bacteria and yeast. This transformation process adds distinct flavors and improves the nutritional value of food in addition to preserving it. Fermentation has long been used to protect foods, including yogurt, kombucha, pickles, kimchi, and sauerkraut. Fermentation offers a low-tech and energy-efficient technique to prolong the life of perishable items while delivering microorganisms that support gut health in off-grid living situations where refrigeration may be scarce.

When it comes to off-grid living, one of the main benefits of canning is its capacity to preserve the harvest during years of abundance for consumption during times of scarcity. Because off-grid agriculture is seasonal, some crops may yield profusely at particular times, necessitating the development of a plan for storing and utilizing the excess. Homesteaders can preserve fruits and vegetables for use later, when the garden may not be as fruitful, by canning them while they are at their peak of freshness and flavor. In line with sustainability and self-sufficiency, this allows off-grid communities to depend on their stored harvest instead of purchasing substitutes from stores.

Canning reduces waste by keeping excess produce from spoiling and improving food's shelf life. Managing the excess produce from gardens and orchards is a common problem for off-grid homesteaders. Canning becomes an invaluable tool when extra fruits and vegetables are turned into pantry staples that can be enjoyed all year long. Off-grid homesteaders can build a resilient food system that reduces waste and optimizes the usefulness of their products by adopting the values of thrift and resourcefulness.

Canning is an excellent option for off-grid living because of its accessibility and simplicity; relying on power and sophisticated technologies might not be feasible. With just a few essential ingredients (jars, lids, a big pot, and a stove), water bath canning is an easy process that may be modified for off-grid kitchens. Although it calls for extra equipment, pressure canning offers a secure method of preserving low-acid foods without sacrificing their nutritious content. This fits well with the off-grid lifestyle's core values of self-sufficiency, simplicity, and low-impact technology.

In addition to addressing the issues of seasonality and surplus, fermentation preserves food and offers off-grid populations particular health advantages. By making vitamins, minerals, and other vital nutrients more bioavailable, fermentation improves the nutritional profile of food. Probiotics, for instance, are abundant in fermented foods like kimchi and sauerkraut and enhance intestinal health as well as immune system function. Fermented dairy products, like kefir and yogurt, have a longer shelf life and serve as a source of good bacteria for gut health.

Fermented foods offer a way to add variety and nutritional richness to the diet in off-grid situations where the availability of fresh vegetables may be limited during certain seasons. Fermenting and storing nutrient-dense foods improves the general health of off-grid homesteaders by encouraging a robust and well-rounded approach to food security.

The diversity of cultures and cuisines linked to fermented foods enhances the complexity of off-grid living. Homesteaders can generate distinctive flavors and textures by experimenting with different fermenting procedures. Fermentation becomes a creative craft.

Endeavor, enabling people to create distinctive ferments using regional ingredients, tastes, and customs. This cultural link to food fosters this rootedness in the homesteading lifestyle and feeling of identity, which enriches the off-grid living experience.

Although canning and fermentation offer many advantages for off-grid life, some drawbacks must be carefully considered. A major obstacle is finding a dependable and secure source for canning jars, lids, and other supplies. Obtaining these goods might be challenging for off-grid homesteaders, particularly in isolated areas. These difficulties can be lessened by employing techniques like reusing jars and lids, finding used equipment, or investigating less specialist techniques like fermentation.

There could be an additional learning curve for off-grid homesteaders who must become more experienced with canning and fermenting. Both methods require expertise, understanding, and focus on details to guarantee the security and caliber of preserved goods. Finding the time and resources for learning and experimenting may necessitate a purposeful commitment to picking up the required skills in off-grid living, where people frequently wear many hats.

It is crucial to guarantee the safety of foods that have been preserved, significantly when canning, as using the wrong methods can increase the danger of botulism. To reduce this risk, off-grid homesteaders must go by set rules, utilize tried-and-true recipes, and follow the proper canning techniques. The preservation process is made more difficult by the need to ensure food safety, which calls for attention to detail and dedication.

Finally, off-grid homesteaders looking to preserve and optimize the usefulness of their produce will find that canning and fermentation are vital resources. These conventional techniques, which align with the ideas of self-sufficiency, waste minimization, and sustainability, tackle the problems of seasonality, surplus, and restricted availability of fresh fruit. Foods that have been canned have a longer shelf life so that homesteaders can rely on their preserved harvest in hard times. Foods that have undergone fermentation retain their nutritional content and improve intestinal health and dietary diversity. The resilience, self-sufficiency, and cultural richness that canning and fermentation bring to off-grid living are clear examples of the transformative power of these practices, even in the face of obstacles like equipment access and the learning curve involved in using them. Off-grid homesteaders capture the essence of the seasons in jars of preserved fruits, vegetables, and fermented treats, guaranteeing a plentiful and varied culinary experience year.

Root Cellars

Off-grid homesteaders can keep perishable produce year-round in a sustainable and energy-efficient manner by using root cellars, a tried-and-true method of food preservation. These underground storage facilities use the Earth's inherent insulating qualities to provide a climate ideal for preserving fruits, vegetables, and other crops long-term. The present discourse delves into the principles, advantages, building techniques, obstacles, and revolutionary influence of root cellars within the framework of off-grid living. It highlights the significance of these structures in fostering food security, mitigating dependence on outside resources, and establishing a connection between homesteaders and the seasonal cycles.

The use of steady, cool subterranean temperatures to

delay the ripening and deterioration of harvested crops is the fundamental idea behind the root cellar concept. Off-grid homesteaders can increase the shelf life of their crops with this natural refrigeration system without using energy or complicated technology. Root cellars are the perfect storage option for off-grid living because they are designed with essential elements like insulation, ventilation, and humidity control in mind.

This creates a climate that resembles the chilly temperatures found in nature.

The capacity of root cellars to offer a steady, cold storage space for a range of crops is one of its main advantages. A well-designed root cellar will keep fruits and vegetables that rot quickly in warmer climates for several months. This makes off-grid homesteads more self-sufficient by extending the time they can rely on their grown vegetables, cutting down on the number of trips to the grocery store, and eliminating food waste.

To achieve maximum performance, a root cellar's construction requires careful consideration of crucial components. The cellar's ability to maintain a constant temperature depends heavily on insulation. Insulators such as straw bales and earth berms are used to reduce temperature swings. Another critical factor is ventilation, which keeps ethylene gas produced by some fruits from building up and accelerating the ripening of nearby products. Vegetables stored must have their humidity controlled adequately, typically accomplished in the cellar using wet sand or water containers.

Root cellar designs and building techniques vary widely, meeting off-grid homesteaders' unique requirements and financial constraints. Traditional underground root cellars, which are buried to use the insulating qualities of soil, are one style frequently seen. An alternative method entails building an above-ground root cellar, which is commonly designed to resemble a little shed and has ventilation and insulation features to simulate the chilly environment of an underground chamber. Numerous considerations must be considered while selecting the best design, including soil type, climate, available space, and the kinds of crops to be stored.

Root cellars are helpful for more than just storing stuff; they help off-grid homesteaders develop a closer bond with the seasons. A year-round supply of homegrown fruits and vegetables is available to homesteaders who harvest produce at its prime and store it in a root cellar by the principles of seasonality. This relationship with the seasons improves the nutritional value of the homestead's food and cultivates a sense of balance with the environment's organic cycles.

Root cellars play a significant role in off-grid food security, which is essential to self-sufficiency. Homesteaders can better endure times of scarcity or dire growing circumstances if they store an excess of crops during times of prosperity. Being resilient is especially important when living off the grid because access to outside resources may be restricted. Thus, root cellars provide off-grid homesteads with a dependable food supply by acting as a cost-effective and practical insurance policy against weather fluctuations.

Root cellars' little environmental impact is consistent with off-grid living's sustainability objectives. Unlike contemporary refrigeration systems, which run on electricity, root cellars use the natural thermal mass of the Earth to produce an excellent storage space. By minimizing dependence on outside power sources, this energy-efficient method lessens the environmental impact of off-grid homesteads. By adopting sustainable practices, off-grid communities support a more resilient and regenerative relationship with their immediate surroundings.

Even with their many advantages, root cellar design, building, and upkeep present particular difficulties. Inadequate ventilation and insulation can lead to imbalances in humidity or temperature, and design mistakes can also cause these problems. Produce stored may freeze or rot due to temperature extremes brought on by inadequate insulation. On the other hand, inadequate ventilation can lead to the accumulation of ethylene gas, hastening the ripening process of fruits and vegetables. A root cellar's construction calls for carefully balancing these aspects to create the best circumstances for storing food for an extended period.

Another problem is determining the best location for a root cellar because factors like drainage, soil composition, and closeness to water tables can affect how well the structure works there. Off-grid homesteaders can confront challenges because of rocky or unstable terrain, necessitating innovative fixes or different layouts. Furthermore, continuous upkeep is necessary to handle problems like pest management, mold avoidance, and the routine inspection of stored goods to eliminate rotting components.

In conclusion, root cellars offer a basic and long-lasting answer for off-grid homesteaders looking to store and preserve their produce. Root cellars' built-in natural refrigeration, insulation, and ventilation systems provide a tried-and-true, low-tech method of storing food. Root cellars are revolutionary in the quest for self-sufficiency because they promote a relationship with the seasons, improve food security, and reduce environmental impact. Root cellars provide off-grid homesteaders with a dependable and durable way to preserve the wealth of their land, even though their design and upkeep present some problems. One season's bounty provides the homestead with sustenance throughout the year, as evidenced by the fruits of the harvest finding a haven in the cool darkness of a well-planned root cellar.

Drying and Smoking Techniques

Food preservation techniques such as drying and smoking have been around for ages and continue to provide off-grid homesteaders with adequate means of extending the shelf life of perishable items. These time- tested methods, rooted in tradition, use air, heat, and time to drive out moisture and stop the growth of spoiling bacteria. When preserving gathered vegetables, meats, and herbs, drying and smoking become indispensable methods in the off-grid living environment, where electricity may be scarce or nonexistent. In the context of off-grid food preservation, this section examines the fundamentals, procedures, advantages, difficulties, and revolutionary effects of drying and smoking processes. It highlights these methods' contributions to improving self-sufficiency, cutting down on waste, and establishing a bond with local culinary customs.

One of the earliest techniques for preserving food is drying, which includes taking the moisture out of food to create an inhospitable atmosphere for microbes. Fish has been air-dried in Scandinavia for thousands of years, while fruits were sun-dried in ancient Egypt—a process that has roots in many different cultures. Dried fruits, vegetables, herbs, and meats become a valuable and energy-efficient way to preserve food when living off the grid, when refrigeration may not always be available. Typically, the procedure entails exposing the food to heat and air until the appropriate amount of moisture is gone. This can be done in the sun, on air-drying racks, or in low-temperature ovens.

The ease of use and accessibility of drying in off-grid living are two of its main advantages. Food can be dried with three simple ingredients: air, sunshine or low heat, and time. This fits perfectly with the off-grid lifestyle's low-tech living and self-sufficiency guiding ideals. Dried foods are an excellent option for off-grid homesteaders who value efficiency and creativity in their food preservation techniques because they are lightweight, take up less storage space, and are portable.

A wide variety of food products can benefit from drying. When fruits and vegetables are dried, their nutrients and flavors are concentrated. While meats take on a portable and shelf-stable shape, dried herbs maintain their gastronomic and fragrant properties. By drying excess produce during prime harvest seasons, off-grid homesteaders can increase their self-sufficiency and diversify their diet while guaranteeing a year-round supply of preserved goods. Dried foods are an essential component of off-grid pantry staples due to their convenience and ability to retain nutrients.

A classic solar-powered approach that demonstrates the coexistence of off-grid living and food preservation is sun drying. Homesteaders living off the grid can organically use solar energy to dry fruits, vegetables, and herbs. This approach lessens reliance on outside resources while preserving the harvest's abundance. Only essential racks or trays are needed for sun drying; the sun's force covers the rest. This is consistent with the off-grid lifestyle philosophy, emphasizing the importance of sustainable behaviors and reliance on renewable energy sources.

While smoking is a preservation method that combines dehydration with smoke's antibacterial qualities, drying mostly concentrates on eliminating moisture. Smoking creates an unfriendly atmosphere for bacteria and fungi, providing unique flavors and functions as a natural preservative. People have used this dual-action method for ages to increase the shelf life of fish and meats. When living off the grid and refrigeration may not be an option, smoking becomes a tasty and effective technique to store protein sources.

There are two popular techniques for smoking meats to preserve them: cold smoking and hot smoking. By exposing meats to smoke without generating heat, cold smoking helps keep the meat's texture and flavor. This technique works well for products like sausages, bacon, and several types of fish. In contrast, hot smoking combines smoke and higher temperatures to flavor and thoroughly cook the meat. A product made using either method can be kept for long periods without refrigeration.

Beyond preservation, smoking has a dramatic effect on off-grid living through the development of culinary delights. The off-grid homesteader's diet gains depth and variety from smoked meats and seafood, giving dishes a distinct and flavorful dimension. Selecting different types of wood to smoke, like mesquite, applewood, or hickory, results in unique flavors that off-grid homesteaders can use to customize their smoking experience and produce signature smoked foods. Smoking turns into a culinary custom that links isolated populations to age-old customs that improve the taste of preserved goods.

There are several advantages for off-grid homesteaders regarding smoking and drying. By preserving perishable items, these methods support food security and sustainability, self-sufficiency, and gastronomic diversity. Off-grid homesteaders can increase the shelf life of their harvests by drying them, providing a consistent supply of nutrient-dense foods all year. Drying is an accessible option for homesteaders looking for workable solutions for their off-grid living because of its simplicity and low requirements.

Furthermore, a critical benefit of drying and smoking food in off-grid life is decreased food waste. Through these approaches, homesteaders can reduce the amount of excess fruits, vegetables, and meats thrown out. This aligns with the off-grid living concept of resource efficiency, which emphasizes maximizing the use of harvested crops and minimizing dependency on outside resources. Desiccating and Off-grid homesteaders need help with drying and smoking since they require specific tools, a particular climate, and close attention to detail. Insect management, air movement, and humidity levels can all affect how well the drying process goes. Even though solar drying requires little technology and energy, off-grid homesteaders may need to help maintain proper drying conditions, particularly in humid locations. Dehydrators and ovens used for indoor drying may need a power source, which might be problematic in remote areas with intermittent electricity.

In conclusion, off-grid living concepts align well with the age-old practices of smoking and drying. Off-grid homesteaders have viable and sustainable options to preserve and improve the flavors of their produce thanks to these preservation techniques. With its ease of use and adaptability, drying enables homesteaders to produce nutrient-dense pantry staples, while smoking gives preserved meats and fish more flavor and depth. Beyond food security, additional advantages include decreased waste, many culinary options, and a stronger bond with cultural customs. Although specific difficulties are mainly related to gear and environmental factors, they are surpassed by how much these methods have changed the off-grid homesteading way of life. Off-grid homesteaders celebrate the abundance of their land and the wisdom of using traditional food preservation methods by enjoying the flavors of the harvest all year long in the rhythmic dance of air, heat, and time.

CHAPTER VIII

Self-Sufficiency in Daily Living

Homemade Products

In off-grid living, handmade goods are essential to sustainability and self-sufficiency. They symbolize a return to traditional ways of life that value creativity, resourcefulness, and a relationship with the land. In the world of off-grid homesteading, where there is less dependence on outside resources, making things yourself turns into a life-changing and liberating experience. In the context of off-grid life, this section examines the fundamentals, processes, advantages, difficulties, and transforming effects of making handmade things. It highlights how these activities promote independence, lessen environmental impact, and develop a feeling of creativity and purpose.

Making necessities by hand, such as food, clothes, cleaning supplies, or personal care items, is the foundation of homemade goods. Creating basics at home becomes a practical necessity when living off the grid since access to commercial items may be limited. Using local resources, lowering reliance on outside supply chains, and limiting the environmental impact of mass production and shipping are all part of creating handmade goods.

In off-grid living, one of the main advantages of handmade goods is the development of self-sufficiency. The goal of off-grid homesteaders is to minimize reliance on outside systems by developing a way of life-based mainly on their abilities and resources. Handcrafted goods, such as bread baking, soap making, or apparel stitching, support this philosophy by enabling people to independently care for their basic requirements. Being self-sufficient becomes a source of pride and fortitude in the face of outside uncertainties, making it more than just a pragmatic consideration.

Making goods from scratch is consistent with the off-grid living tenets of sustainability and environmental stewardship. Off-grid homesteaders can reduce their reliance on industrially produced commodities, which can have high environmental costs, by making things home. The carbon footprint of production and transportation operations is reduced when handmade products are manufactured using natural and local materials. Avoiding throwaway things and single-use packaging also cuts waste, which supports a more ecologically conscious and regenerative way of living.

The various handcrafted goods used in off-grid living encompass many facets of day-to-day existence. Regarding food, off-grid homesteaders frequently create their dairy products from on-site cattle, bake their bread, and preserve their fruits. Producing one's food strengthens a person's bond with the land and the seasons while also guaranteeing its quality and freshness. Similarly, making your cleaning solutions at home with essential items like vinegar and baking soda helps you live a better and greener lifestyle by reducing your reliance on commercial, chemical-filled goods.

Moreover, homemade personal care items highlight the ease of use and adaptability of off-grid living. Off-grid homesteaders frequently use natural substances like herbs, essential oils, and beeswax to make soaps, shampoos, and lotions. This prevents artificial chemicals from being included in many commercial items and permits customization based on personal preferences. Handcrafted personal care products symbolize the homesteader's dedication to their health, well-being, and a more balanced coexistence with the environment.

Another aspect of off-grid living that reflects the ethos of self-reliance is the manufacture of handmade textiles and clothes. Homesteaders living off the grid might grow their flax for linen, raise their sheep for wool, or upcycle old textiles into new clothing. Handmade textiles are an art form that connects people living off the grid to traditional crafts that have supported their communities for generations through techniques like spinning, weaving, and stitching. In addition to allowing for self-expression, handmade clothing lessens dependency on the fashion industry's resource-intensive and frequently exploitative practices.

Gaining and perfecting the required abilities and knowledge is often the first step toward producing handmade goods in an off-grid setting. Learning ancient skills like weaving, soap-making, and bread-baking takes time, patience, and commitment. Off-grid homesteaders may encounter a learning curve when acquiring these abilities, particularly if they are starting. Additionally, there may be logistical difficulties in procuring the supplies and tools needed for some handcrafted items, especially in isolated, off-grid areas with limited access to specialist resources.

The profoundly transformational effect of handmade products on off-grid living persists despite the hurdles. Beyond the obvious advantages of sustainability and self-sufficiency, making homemade products becomes a fulfilling endeavor. Off-grid homesteaders experience a closer bond with their everyday lives as they work directly to produce goods that enhance and support their way of life. For instance, creating bread turns the kitchen into a hub of creativity and nourishment, where flour, water, and yeast produce a household staple.

Creating a distinctive and customized way of life while living off the grid is further enhanced by using handmade goods. Individual beliefs, tastes, and priorities are reflected in the decisions made when producing items at home. The practical and decorative qualities of handmade goods grow to represent the homesteader's individuality and create a unique living space that speaks to sincerity and purpose. The off-grid house gains character and a personal touch from handcrafted goods, such as the texture of hand-knit socks, freshly brewed herbal tea, or the warmth of a handmade quilt.

In addition, producing goods from scratch encourages sharing and a sense of community among off-grid dwellers. Knowledge and abilities are shared among neighbors or passed down through the generations, forming a network of support for one another. In the off-grid society, exchanging handmade things develops into a kind of barter and cooperation that fortifies social ties and promotes a sense of interconnectivity. The cooperative nature of making things by hand is consistent with the community mentality prevalent in off-grid living, where pooled resources and expertise promote all welfare.

In summary, handmade goods are more than just valuable essentials for off-grid living; they represent a way of life emphasizing sustainability, creativity, and self-sufficiency. Making things at home supports cutting waste, minimizing the environmental impact, and developing a distinctive and purposeful way of living. The transformative influence on an off-grid homesteader's sense of purpose, connection to the land, and ability to contribute to a more resilient and sustainable community outweighs the challenges of learning new skills and gathering supplies. Off-grid homesteaders find physical manifestations of a meaningful and holistic way of life in handmade items like bread, candles, and clothing created by hand.

Health and Wellness Practices

Health and wellness practices are profoundly relevant in off-grid living, where people value self-sufficiency, overall well-being, and a harmonious relationship with the natural environment. Off-grid homesteaders participate in various unconventional health and wellness activities to live a robust and healthy lifestyle. In the framework of off-grid living, this section examines the tenets, strategies, advantages, difficulties, and transforming power of health and wellness activities. It highlights the contributions these practices make to promoting mental clarity, physical vigor, and a strong sense of connectedness to the cycles of nature.

Integrating spiritual, mental, and physical wellbeing is the cornerstone of a holistic approach to health and wellness in off-grid life. Off-grid homesteaders frequently lead physically demanding lives, engage in outdoor pursuits, and consume a diet high in whole, locally produced foods. Daily chores, such as building and maintaining structures or caring for gardens and animals, take on a rhythm that serves as a functional exercise that enhances general health. This focus on physical activity is consistent with sustainability and self-sufficiency, transforming everyday tasks into chances for physical health.

Whole, nutrient-dense foods are prioritized in off-grid life, where nutrition is the cornerstone of health and wellness. Growing fruits, vegetables, and herbs at home make a diet high in vitamins, minerals, and antioxidants possible. Homesteaders living off the grid frequently employ organic and regenerative farming methods instead of artificial chemicals or pesticides. Growing and harvesting one's food cultivates a strong bond with the land and an understanding of how seasonal patterns influence dietary decisions. Off-grid people prioritize a diet rich in nutrients and procured locally by minimizing their reliance on processed and commercially manufactured foods.

An essential aspect of living off the grid is mental and physical health. The absence of urban noise, the serenity of rural settings, and being surrounded by nature all contribute to a calm and stress-relieving atmosphere. Homesteaders living off the grid frequently find comfort in the routine simplicity of their lives, away from the rush and bustle of contemporary society. Living in balance with nature becomes a healing practice promoting emotional fortitude, cerebral clarity, and a deep sense of serenity.

Meditation and contemplation are two practices that are well-suited to the serenity of off-grid areas and further promote mindfulness and mental resilience. People can better tune into their inner thoughts and feelings when there aren't continual external stimuli present, which fosters self-awareness and emotional health. A mental anchor and a sense of inner balance are fostered by meditation, which becomes a tool for managing the difficulties of off-grid living amid the uncertainties and responsibilities of farming.

Being in tune with nature is essential to health and well-being in off-grid life. People frequently spend much time outside, whether hiking, tending to gardening, or just taking in the scenery. Outdoor activities provide many opportunities for sun exposure, an essential vitamin D source, and promote mental and physical well-being. When living off the grid, maintaining a connection to nature is not only a backdrop but an active component of the quest for health and wellbeing.

Off-grid living frequently incorporates hydrotherapy, another natural health technique, by building natural swimming ponds, taking cold plunges in natural water sources, or using outdoor showers. These activities offer a direct and energizing connection to the elements and enhance the immune system and circulation to promote physical wellness. The benefits of cold water immersion therapy are welcomed by off-grid homesteaders who align with sustainable health practices and natural living ideals.

Herbalism and natural medicine are holistic health methods used in off-grid life. Many off-grid homesteaders grow plants and herbs for medicinal purposes, turning their property into a pharmacy. Herbal treatments serve as a first line of treatment for common illnesses, supporting self-sufficiency and lowering the need for pharmacological interventions. An essential aspect of an off-grid homesteader's toolset for keeping well and curing minor ailments is their understanding of indigenous flora and their therapeutic uses.

Off-grid living has many advantages regarding health and fitness, but there are drawbacks that should be carefully considered. Remote off-grid areas may have limited access to healthcare services; therefore, taking proactive steps to maintain good health is necessary. Off-grid homesteaders frequently keep emergency communication plans, stock their cabinets with herbal remedies, and engage in first aid training. Off-grid living's intrinsic self-reliance extends to health care, necessitating a certain amount of readiness and fortitude in the face of difficulties.

Furthermore, although the physical demands of off-grid life can improve general fitness, they can also cause problems with joint health and muscular tension. If appropriate procedures and safeguards are not used, manual labor, heavy lifting, and repetitive chores can result in overuse injuries. To preserve joint flexibility and muscle strength, off-grid people need to weigh the advantages of physical activity against a knowledge of body mechanics. They can do this by adding exercises like yoga, stretching, or focused workouts.

To sum up, health and wellness practices are the cornerstone of a lifestyle that prioritizes self-sufficiency, overall wellbeing, and a peaceful coexistence with nature rather than merely being an add-on to off-grid living. Combining physical work, whole food diet, mindfulness, and interaction with the natural world creates a holistic approach to health that goes beyond traditional thinking. Obstacles like the physical demands of homesteading and the lack of access to healthcare are overcome with fortitude, readiness, and a dedication to a way of life that puts the entire possible emphasis on wellbeing. Off-grid life creates a tapestry where health and wellness practices are interwoven with mental toughness, physical energy, and a deep connection to the natural world's cycles.

Skill Development

In the dynamic world of off-grid living, where people travel towards self-sufficiency, resilience, and a connection to traditional crafts, skill development is paramount. Off-grid homesteaders understand the value of developing a broad range of skills, from artisanal to practical, to live a lifestyle that reduces the need for outside systems. In the context of off-grid life, this section examines the fundamentals, strategies, advantages, difficulties, and revolutionary effects of skill development, highlighting its function in promoting self- sufficiency, flexibility, and preserving necessary knowledge.

Self-sufficiency is the fundamental tenet of off-grid life, and developing one's skills becomes the way for people to attain a certain degree of independence in providing for their own needs. Off-grid homesteaders create a toolkit of abilities that enables them to deal with the difficulties of living in distant or rural areas, from building and construction to food preservation. A few examples of practical talents that enable off-grid people to build and maintain their homes, cultivate their food, and efficiently manage their resources are carpentry, plumbing, electrical work, and gardening.

The development of adaptation is one of the main advantages of off-grid living skill development. Off-grid homesteaders frequently encounter circumstances where conventional remedies are more appropriate than contemporary comforts. The capacity to fix a damaged tool, build a temporary shelter, or solve a technical problem becomes crucial when access to expert services can be restricted. Gaining new skills gives people the adaptability they need to succeed in various challenging and occasionally unpredictably changing situations.

Moreover, the development of off-grid living skills is consistent with environmental care and sustainability values. Local materials and renewable resources are frequently used in traditional crafts and skills. Working with wood, stone, or natural fibers teaches people about the ecological context of their environment and cultivates a profound respect for the land's resources. Off-grid homesteaders support the preservation of artisanal knowledge that may otherwise be lost in the era of mass production by prioritizing skill development in these fields.

Beyond just being functional, skill development has a transforming effect that helps preserve cultural history and promote a feeling of community. Customary arts and crafts, like weaving, ceramics, and blacksmithing, have a rich past beyond individual homesteads. Acquiring and transmitting these abilities constitute cultural perpetuity, uniting the current generation with the knowledge and customs of the past. Off-grid communities build networks of information sharing and mutual support within the spirit of skill sharing.

Off-grid living fosters the development of practical skills related to agricultural techniques, animal husbandry, and food production. A self-sufficient lifestyle includes gardening, rearing livestock, and preserving crops using techniques like fermentation or canning. Acquiring proficiency in these domains guarantees a consistent and varied food supply and strengthens the homesteader's bond with the natural cycles. When knowledgeable about seasonal planting, animal care, and food storage, nourishment becomes a dynamic and collaborative relationship with the earth.

Off-grid life frequently promotes the development of artistic and creative capabilities in addition to practical ones. Making things by hand, such as furniture, clothes, or ceramics, becomes an artistic endeavor in addition to meeting practical demands. Off-grid homesteaders add a personal touch to their projects, giving commonplace items a sense of character and significance. Building one's skills through artisanal crafts becomes a creative and self-discovery journey that fits well with meaningful and purposeful living ideas.

While learning to live off the grid has many advantages, some drawbacks call for commitment and tenacity. Learning new talents comes with a learning curve that takes patience and time, primarily if they are based on traditional crafts. Off-grid homesteaders who go into the complexities of carpentry, animal husbandry, or other crafts may encounter obstacles and disappointments. Nevertheless, these difficulties are essential to learning, and conquering them builds resilience and a sense of success.

Furthermore, combining ancient abilities with modern technologies presents a particular difficulty for off-grid life. Some occupations demand a balance between old knowledge and modern tools, while others, like carpentry or gardening, are ageless and ideal for off-grid living. For instance, solar energy requires knowledge of contemporary renewable energy systems and conventional electrical operations. Finding the perfect mix between traditional methods and modern innovations is a complex part of learning to live off the grid.

Developing skills related to off-grid life has a profound effect that extends beyond individual homesteads and fosters a culture of information sharing and mutual assistance within communities. People can learn from one another through workshops, skill-sharing gatherings, and mentorship programs, which promote the growth of a dynamic knowledge ecosystem. The cooperative nature of skill development is consistent with the community mentality prevalent in off-grid communities, where pooled resources and knowledge enhance the well-being of all members.

To sum up, learning how to live off the grid is a transforming process that involves artisanal, communal, and practical aspects. It is not only a necessary skill. Gaining abilities opens doors to flexibility, independence, and preserving the required knowledge. Difficulties encountered during the learning process are tackled with resolve and a dedication to resilience. Off-grid homesteaders create a way of life emphasizing self-sufficiency, cultural continuity, and peaceful coexistence with the natural environment as they develop various skills. Skill development in off-grid living becomes a monument to the transforming power of knowledge and the tenacity of people dedicated to blazing their route in embracing self-sufficient life in the hands that create, the tools that craft, and the brains that learn.

CHAPTER IX

Off-Grid Technology Integration

Communication Solutions

Off-grid life is when individuals attempt to establish communication, collaboration, and access to information in locations disconnected from the grid or where they are self-sufficient. Communication solutions are essential in this context. Off-grid homesteaders are motivated to investigate novel communication tactics because they face constraints such as geographical remoteness, limited infrastructure, and a desire to be self-sufficient. This section explores the principles, methods, benefits, challenges, and transformative impact of communication solutions within the context of off-grid living. Particular attention is paid to these solutions' role in fostering community, enabling emergency preparedness, and bridging the gap between traditional lifestyles and modern connectivity.

Establishing dependable ways of interacting with the outside world is at the heart of the communication solutions required for off-grid life. Traditional methods such as two-way radios, satellite phones, and landline telephones play an essential role when circumventing the constraints of cellular networks in remote locations. Homesteaders who live off the grid frequently invest in communication systems not dependent on external infrastructure. This means that they can maintain connections with their neighbors, emergency services, and the larger community. In locations not connected to the grid, the capacity to communicate is not merely a convenience; instead, it is an essential component of both safety and well-being.

Off-grid life has been increasingly widespread in recent years, and with it has come the incorporation of contemporary technology, particularly the internet, which has provided them with transformative communication alternatives. The use of satellite internet, in particular, enables homesteaders not linked to the grid to gain access to online resources, operate remotely, and maintain connections with worldwide networks. The pragmatic incorporation of internet access corresponds with the increasing demands and goals of persons seeking a balance between self-sufficiency and modern communication. Traditionalists may argue that off-grid life should involve a complete withdrawal from modern amenities; however, this is not the case.

In addition, social media and online platforms play a part in developing a sense of community among homesteaders who live off the grid. Even though geographical obstacles exist, virtual spaces offer platforms for the exchange of information, the sharing of skills, and the provision of mutual assistance. Individuals can interact with one another, work together, and share their experiences through these digital communities, which helps to alleviate the feeling of isolation often associated with living off the grid. Individuals who share a similar lifestyle and are interested in building a sense of belonging and camaraderie can do so through the virtual environment, which serves as a location for such activities.

Off-grid life requires several important considerations, one of which is emergency readiness. In times of disaster, effective communication solutions are of the utmost importance. Homesteaders who live off the grid frequently devise communication plans that cover a wide range of potential outcomes, including medical emergencies, natural disasters, and other unanticipated occurrences. Individuals can coordinate their responses, seek aid, and protect the community's safety by accessing two-way radios, satellite phones, and designated meeting spots as part of an all-encompassing emergency communication strategy.

Messages conveyed by hand, signaling systems, and community gatherings are all examples of alternate communication methods that can be utilized in off-grid living. Since interpersonal interactions are highly prized in small and intimate off-grid communities, reliance on face-to-face communication becomes a strength in these societies. Communicating information through direct interactions helps cultivate a sense of togetherness and shared responsibility, which in turn contributes to the community's resilience in the face of adversities.

Despite the numerous advantages, there are obstacles to deploying communication solutions in off-grid life. Radio transmissions can be disrupted by geographical impediments, such as high terrain or dense forests, which might reduce the efficiency of specific communication instruments. While satellite internet services do provide connectivity, there is a possibility that they contain latency difficulties or that they are susceptible to disturbances caused by the weather. It is necessary to carefully analyze one's interests and financial limits to determine whether the initial expenditures of acquiring satellite phones or other specialized communication devices are prohibitive for specific individuals.

In addition, incorporating contemporary communication technologies into off-grid living raises problems regarding the potential influence this may have on the traditional rhythms and ideals of the lifestyle. Some people who live off the grid and homestead may be reluctant to accept internet connectivity. They may express concerns about the incursion of foreign influences and the destruction of the self-sufficient belief system. For individuals navigating the convergence of technology and off-grid living, finding a way to strike a balance between the benefits of modern communication and the preservation of traditional values becomes a subtle concern.

When it comes to off-grid life, the transformative influence of communication solutions is visible in communities' increased connectivity, collaboration, and resilience. A sense of collective empowerment can be attributed to exchanging information, requesting support, and coordinating actions by sharing knowledge. An effective communication system becomes a lifeline in times of emergency because it enables individuals to respond quickly and ensures the safety of the community as a whole. The combination of contemporary technology and more conventional modes of communication is an example of a dynamic adaptation to the ever-changing requirements of homesteaders who live off the utility grid.

In conclusion, communication solutions are essential in the fabric of off-grid living because they bridge the gap between self-sufficiency and connectedness. Homesteaders who live off the grid must overcome the hurdles of remoteness and limited infrastructure to establish dependable communication channels. These challenges can be overcome through traditional means like two-way radios, landlines, or modern satellite internet. The transformative influence goes beyond simple connectivity, as it helps cultivate a feeling of community, makes it possible to be prepared for emergencies, and contributes to the resilience of those seeking a lifestyle that strikes a balance between self-sufficiency and the advantages of contemporary communication. In off-grid life, communication solutions become threads that weave a tapestry of connectedness, collaboration, and shared experiences. This is accomplished through the combination of traditional ideals with modern tools.

Internet Options

In the world of off-grid living, where the pursuit of self-sufficiency coexists with the need for connectivity, the availability of internet options plays a vital role in defining the lifestyle choices of persons looking to bridge the gap between traditional practices and modern conveniences. Off-grid homesteaders are motivated to investigate various internet connectivity options because they face constraints brought on by geographical isolation, limited infrastructure, and a determination to make their lives more environmentally friendly. In this section, we delve into the fundamentals, methods, advantages, disadvantages, and transformative impact of internet options within the context of off-grid living. We highlight the role these internet options play in facilitating communication, enabling remote work, and navigating the delicate balance between technological connectivity and preserving a self-sufficient ethos.

Satellite internet is a game-changing solution that comes at the junction of living off the grid and accessing the Internet. In contrast to more conventional networks such as cable or fiber-optic connections, Satellite internet depends on communication satellites that circle the Earth. It is especially well-suited for use in off-grid and isolated areas, where installing physical cables could be impractical or prohibitively expensive. This approach has a broader reach and is particularly useful for such settings. Internet via satellite provides homesteaders not connected to the grid access to various online resources, communication platforms, and even the opportunity to work remotely. Satellite internet access gives new opportunities for people who want to live off the grid but enjoy the advantages of contemporary communication. This is because satellite internet access allows users to connect to the Internet.

The fact that satellite internet is accessible to everyone is one of the most significant advantages of living off the grid. The traditional infrastructure of the Internet typically involves a considerable investment in the laying of cables or the establishment of ground-based towers, which makes it economically impractical in parts of the country that are geographically isolated. In contrast, satellite internet can overcome geographical constraints, making it possible to link even the most remote off-grid homesteads to the Internet. Due to this inclusion, individuals are given the flexibility to live a self-sufficient lifestyle without compromising their capacity to access online information, connect with the outside world, and participate in virtual communities.

Additionally, satellite internet is compatible with the ideals of resiliency and emergency preparedness associated with off-grid living options. In times of crisis, when conventional communication infrastructure may be compromised, satellite internet remains a dependable means of maintaining connectivity. Homesteaders who live off the grid frequently encounter problems such as unforeseen events, natural disasters, or medical emergencies, requiring prompt communication and access to information. The use of satellite internet becomes an essential resource in these circumstances since it enables individuals to coordinate their responses, seek aid, and ensure that the community is safe.

Satellite internet in off-grid living settings presents several obstacles, even though it offers several benefits. For users participating in real-time activities such as online gaming or meetings, latency, which refers to the amount of time that passes between sending and receiving data, can be a cause for concern. Even if they are uncommon, disruptions caused by the weather can affect the satellite signal, which in turn can impact the reliability of the internet connection. Furthermore, the initial expenses of purchasing satellite internet equipment and its monthly membership fees may be exorbitant for some off-grid homesteaders. This necessitates careful consideration of the financial restrictions that an individual may be facing.

The incorporation of satellite internet into off-grid living raises worries regarding the potential impact that it may have on the traditional rhythms and ideals of the lifestyle. Some people who live off the grid may voice concerns about the incursion of external influences, the potential distraction posed by online activities, and the deterioration of the self-sufficient attitude. Those who are negotiating the convergence of technology and off-grid living must take into mind the nuanced consideration of the delicate balance that must be maintained between embracing modern conveniences and retaining the deliberate, self-sustained existence.

In addition to satellite internet, homesteaders who live off the grid investigate several other internet possibilities that align with their commitment to self-sufficiency and sustainability. Mesh networks, for instance, use a decentralized method, which enables users to establish their own local networks without having to rely on any external infrastructure. This method is beneficial in communities not connected to the grid since it allows residents to share internet access within the network, thus significantly decreasing the requirement for individual satellite dishes or other external connections. Mesh networks manifest the communal spirit that is frequently observed in off-grid living. They encourage cooperation and the sharing of resources among residential communities.

Additionally, homesteaders who live off the grid may communicate via low-tech or traditional ways, reducing their dependency on internet services provided by third parties. Within the off-grid community, the dissemination of information might take place through the use of hand-delivered messages, community bulletin boards, or local publications. Cultivating a close-knit, face-to-face communication style characteristic of many off-grid communities is facilitated by these tactics, which not only accord with the principles of self-sufficiency but also contribute to the development of similar communication styles.

The greater connectedness, communication, and access to information that persons experience due to the availability of internet alternatives in off-grid life is a clear indication of the transformative influence of these options. Satellite internet and other alternatives are currently widely utilized to bridge the gap between the benefits of contemporary technology and the self-sufficient lifestyle. One of the factors that adds to a sense of empowerment and adaptability among off-grid homesteaders is the capacity to maintain connections with the outside world, participate in online networks, and gain access to online resources.

In conclusion, the internet alternatives available to those who live off the grid illustrate a dynamic interaction between the necessity for connectivity and the desire to be self-sufficient. As a result of its inclusiveness and robustness, satellite internet emerges as a transformative option that enables off-grid homesteaders to overcome the obstacles of isolation while maintaining their connection to the digital world. Individuals have extra avenues to modify their internet access to correspond with the values and priorities of off-grid life. This can be accomplished using alternative options such as mesh networks or low-tech communication methods. In the delicate dance between technology connectivity and preserving a self-sufficient ethos, internet alternatives become a tool for off-grid homesteaders to design a lifestyle that combines autonomy and connection, tradition and innovation.

Adapting Technology to Homesteading

Homesteading is a subtle and revolutionary approach to off-grid life, where the quest for self-sufficiency crosses with the benefits of modern innovation. Adapting technology to homesteading reflects this intersection. Technology becomes a dynamic force that augments traditional traditions, boosts efficiency, and supports sustainability as individuals embrace the challenges and rewards of homesteading. This occurs as individuals embrace the homesteading lifestyle. This section looks into the fundamentals, methods, benefits, obstacles, and transformative influence of incorporating technology into homesteading. We investigate how the combination of traditional skills and modern equipment can result in a lifestyle that is both harmonious and durable.

One of the most important aspects of incorporating technology into homesteading is acknowledging that traditional abilities and contemporary technologies can coexist in a mutually beneficial way. Homesteading, which focuses on self-sufficiency, sustainable practices, and a connection to the land, is congruent with the philosophy of employing technology as a tool rather than becoming dependent on it. Technology provides answers that improve the efficiency and efficacy of homesteading methods without compromising the fundamental principles of purposeful living. These solutions can be found in agriculture, energy, communication, and infrastructure.

Technology is an essential component in the field of agriculture, as it helps to maximize the production of crops, the raising of livestock, and the administration of resources. Precision agriculture is a modern farming method that makes use of technology. It allows homesteaders to monitor the state of the soil, watch the weather patterns, and use data-driven decision-making for crop management. Irrigation systems that are automated and equipped with sensors and timers provide optimum water use, reducing the amount of wasted water while simultaneously fostering optimal plant growth. Additionally, developments in greenhouse technology have extended the growing season, enabling homesteaders to plant a more excellent range of crops throughout the year. This, in turn, improves both food security and diversity overall.

The integration of technology extends to livestock management, where homesteaders can remotely monitor the health of animals through intelligent monitoring systems, GPS tracking, and health sensors. These gadgets offer real-time data on a variety of aspects, including feeding patterns, health indicators, and location, which enables healthcare providers to give preventative care and respond quickly to any possible problems that may arise. When applied to homesteading, where the health and productivity of the animals that live on the homestead are essential to the long-term viability of the lifestyle, technical improvements of this kind become extremely helpful in assuring the well-being and production of the animals who reside there.

One of the most critical aspects of homesteading is achieving energy independence, and technology plays a vital role in harnessing renewable energy sources. Homesteaders who live off the grid have the opportunity to generate energy that is both clean and sustainable through the use of solar panels, wind turbines, and micro-hydrogenic systems. To overcome the intermittent nature of renewable sources, recent developments in energy storage technology, such as lithium-ion batteries, have made it possible to store extra energy effectively for later use without compromising efficiency. Not only does incorporating these technologies lessen dependency on conventional power grids, but it also leads to the development of a robust and sustainable energy infrastructure that can be adapted to meet the specific requirements of any individual homestead.

One example of how technology might be adapted to fit the off-grid lifestyle is developing communication solutions designed explicitly for homesteading. In remote areas where traditional connectivity may be limited, dependable communication channels can be provided via satellite internet, two-way radios, and mesh networks. These technologies make it easier to be prepared for emergencies and to coordinate with the community and make it possible to interact with online communities, have access to knowledge, and take part in chances to work remotely. Homesteaders can bridge the gap between disconnection and connectivity by incorporating technology into their communication practices. This allows them to enrich their life with the advantages of modern information sharing.

The growth of infrastructure in homesteading also benefits from technological adaptation. Innovations in building, water management, and waste disposal all contribute to an increase in the effectiveness and sustainability of off-grid life. Prefabricated structures, which incorporate energy-efficient designs and environmentally friendly materials, lessen the impact of construction on the environment while simultaneously delivering comfortable and long-lasting housing. Rainwater harvesting systems, greywater recycling, and composting toilets are examples of technology solutions that can be used to conserve water and manage waste. These solutions are in line with the values of environmental stewardship and sustainability.

However, even though there are significant advantages to incorporating technology into homesteading, problems must be carefully considered. Some homesteaders may find themselves in a position where they are unable to afford the upfront costs of acquiring technology, such as solar panels, monitoring systems, or modern tools. Furthermore, the learning curve associated with adopting new technologies requires time and attention, particularly for individuals with minimal technical experience regarding the subject matter. It is necessary to strike a balance between the ease that technology provides and the possible interruptions it may cause to the intentional and hands-on character of traditional activities to incorporate technology into the rhythm of homesteading life successfully.

Adapting technology to homesteading has the potential to have a transformative impact that goes beyond the practical concerns involved and has the potential to change the fundamental essence of the lifestyle. Technology transforms into a tool for empowerment, enabling homesteaders to overcome obstacles, improve efficiency, and expand their repertoire of options. Technology becomes a method of encouraging resilience, sustainability, and a harmonious relationship with the natural world when it is in the hands of individuals who are committed to living an intentional life. The versatility of homesteaders in accepting technology exemplifies the dynamic interplay between tradition and innovation, demonstrating the potential for a lifestyle that includes the best aspects of both the traditional and the modern worlds.

In conclusion, adapting technology to homesteading is a multi-faceted activity encompassing the combination of contemporary innovation and traditional customs. Technology has become a complementary force that promotes the resilience, efficiency, and sustainability of off-grid living. This is true across various applications, including precision agriculture, renewable energy, communication solutions, and infrastructure development. The transformative impact of technology in homesteading extends beyond practical solutions to encompass a philosophy that values adaptation, empowerment, and the harmonious coexistence of old and new.

This is even though there are challenges involved. world skills and contemporary tools. A lifestyle that is both anchored in the past and equipped for the future is crafted by homesteaders through the marriage of tradition and innovation. This lifestyle exemplifies the dynamic synergy between technology and choices that lifestyle are considered purposeful.

CHAPTER X

Financial Strategies for Homesteaders

Budgeting

In the context of off-grid living, budgeting is special because individuals are attempting to manage resources, strategically allocate monies, and create financial resilience to achieve self-sufficiency. When it comes to the delicate dance of purposeful living, where the rhythms of nature, sustainability practices, and the desire for autonomy all collide, budgeting becomes an essential tool for aligning financial goals with the values inherent in off-grid lifestyles. This section investigates the principles, methods, benefits, challenges, and transformative impact of budgeting in the realm of off- grid living. Particular attention is paid to the role that budgeting plays in fostering fiscal responsibility, facilitating long-term planning, and cultivating a balanced relationship between financial considerations and the pursuit of intentional living.

When it comes down to it, budgeting for off-grid living is all about allocating financial resources in such a way that they can accommodate the many requirements of a subsistence lifestyle. A comprehensive evaluation of both short-term and long-term financial goals is the first step in the process. This evaluation considers various factors, including the acquisition of property, the development of infrastructure, the implementation of renewable energy systems, the production of food, and the preparation of emergency plans. Because off-grid living is characterized by its seasonal and changeable nature, whereby one's income may be erratic, and one's expenses may fluctuate in tandem with the cycles of homesteading, budgeting becomes a dynamic tool that can be utilized to adapt to the ever-changing requirements of intentional living.

Off-grid living is characterized by individuals who strive to reduce financial waste, prioritize requirements, and create an attitude of conscious consumerism. One of the most important aspects of budgeting in this lifestyle is this commitment to fiscal responsibility. Homesteaders who live off the grid are encouraged to embrace a modest lifestyle and refrain from making unnecessary purchases as part of the self-sufficiency philosophy, which extends to their financial practices. Individuals can develop their financial resources and lessen their dependency on external financial institutions by carefully examining every expense and making well-informed decisions regarding their purchases. This is in line with the concepts of deliberate and sustainable living.

Planning for the long term is an essential component of budgeting in off-grid living, a lifestyle in which individuals strive to construct a robust and self-sufficient lifestyle. The allocation of finances for the purchase of land, the creation of infrastructure, and the installation of renewable energy systems involves careful consideration of both the immediate demands and the long-term goals being pursued. The creation of a budget serves as a road map for achieving long-term objectives, allowing homesteaders to make gradual progress toward establishing a self-sufficient and sustainable homestead. When it comes to turning fantasies of off-grid life into actual and attainable milestones, the budget becomes a tool that can be utilized for activities such as investing in solar panels, installing rainwater gathering systems, or establishing infrastructure for food production.

In the context of off-grid living, the advantages of budgeting go beyond the management of money resources and cover a more comprehensive approach to deliberate living. Integrating individuals' financial actions with their values can be accomplished by allocating monies to support behaviors that promote sustainability. As a result of this connection between budgeting and values, a sense of purpose and intentionality is created. Every financial decision becomes a step towards developing a lifestyle that reflects a dedication to self-sufficiency, environmental stewardship, and a harmonious relationship with the natural world.

It is necessary to have a sophisticated grasp of the specific situations and variables inherent in purposeful lifestyles to overcome the challenges that arise during budgeting for off-grid living. Traditional budgeting methods may be challenged by factors such as the unpredictable nature of revenue, swings during the seasons, and the initial costs connected with the creation of infrastructure. Homesteaders who live off the grid frequently have to adopt budgeting strategies that are flexible enough to meet the fluctuation of their financial conditions. This budgeting style allows modifications to be made based on the rhythms of homesteading living.

Additionally, the learning curve connected with moving to live off the grid may affect the decisions made regarding budgeting. Those new to the concept of purposeful living may find themselves confronted with unanticipated costs or may misjudge the financial requirements of establishing a self-sufficient farm. It is necessary to be willing to adapt, gain knowledge from experiences, and develop economical methods per the ever-changing requirements and difficulties of off-grid living to build budgeting abilities effectively.

The empowerment, resilience, and intentional decisions that individuals cultivate as a result of budgeting in off-grid living are clear indicators of the significantly transforming impact that budgeting has. When homesteaders use budgeting as a tool for financial empowerment, they can take charge of their economic destinies and lessen their dependence on external financial institutions. Self-sufficiency is a philosophy in which individuals intentionally invest in the development of their homesteads, value sustainability, and construct a lifestyle that is intentional and financially responsible. The ability to make deliberate choices about spending is in line with this philosophy.

In addition, budgeting can develop resilience in the face of economic uncertainty and obstacles that were not anticipated. Off-grid homesteaders have a greater capacity for financial resilience when they can carefully deploy finances for emergency readiness, unanticipated expenses, and changes in revenue. When individuals are better equipped to weather economic storms and continue their pathways toward self-sufficiency, budgeting becomes a proactive technique for navigating the uncertainties of intentional living. This ensures that individuals are better able to sustain themselves financially.

The conclusion is that budgeting in off-grid life is not only a tool for managing finances; it is a revolutionary approach to deliberate living that connects financial goals with the ideals inherent in self-sufficiency and sustainability. One way in which individuals incorporate budgeting into the very fabric of intentional living is by intentionally allocating cash, reducing financial waste, and planning for both urgent needs and long-term objectives. The transformational impact of budgeting extends beyond finance to empower individuals, create resilience, and facilitate a balanced relationship between financial considerations and the pursuit of intentional living. Despite the challenges that budgeting presents, it is a transformative tool. Budgeting serves as a guide, a roadmap, and a method for individuals to design a lifestyle that symbolizes their values and objectives in the domain of off-grid living. This is accomplished through the dance between budgetary responsibility and conscious choices.

Income Generation

In off-grid living, income generation is a dynamic and multidimensional undertaking. Individuals attempt to establish sustainable sources of money that match the concepts of self-sufficiency, resilience, and purposeful living for themselves and their communities. Off-grid homesteaders frequently investigate various methods for earning revenue to achieve their goal of living a lifestyle that is as independent as possible from external systems. These methods range from using conventional farming methods to utilizing contemporary technology to create opportunities for remote labor. This section investigates the principles, methods, benefits, challenges, and transformative impact of income generation in the realm of off-grid living. Particular attention is paid to income generation's role in fostering financial independence, supporting homestead development, and navigating the delicate balance between economic viability and intentional living.

Regarding off-grid living, the realization that financial self-sufficiency is essential to a sustainable lifestyle lies at the heart of generating money. The establishment of homesteads, the building of infrastructure, and the accomplishment of self-sufficiency frequently call for the availability of financial resources. Off-grid homesteaders provide themselves the ability to support the growth of their homesteads, invest in environmentally friendly technologies, and construct a stable economic foundation that complements their deliberate living choices when they actively seek ways to generate income.

The use of traditional farming practices significantly influences the creation of income for homesteaders who live off the grid. Homesteaders use their connection to the land to generate things that may be sold or exchanged via various activities, including the cultivation of crops and the keeping of livestock. Not only does this give a source of income, but it also ensures that the principles of self-sufficiency and sustainability are adhered to. Homesteaders can develop a connection between their livelihoods and the world's natural cycles by selling surplus food, honey, eggs, or handcrafted crafts. This allows them to interact with local marketplaces, support their communities, and establish a business relationship with the natural world.

The advent of technology has made it possible for off-grid homesteaders to take advantage of remote employment opportunities, which have become increasingly feasible. These opportunities allow them to capitalize on their skills and knowledge while preserving their livelihood's independence. Individuals can engage in activities that generate revenue without the requirement for a traditional office setting by working in fields such as writing, graphic design, programming, and online consultancy. The off-grid philosophy is well aligned with this shift toward location-independent labor, which gives homesteaders the flexibility to strike a balance between the demands of homesteading life and the generation of money.

The generation of money in off-grid living has a revolutionary impact that reaches beyond economics and influences the fabric of deliberate living. The attainment of financial independence allows individuals to make conscious decisions regarding their lifestyles, emphasize sustainability, and navigate the precarious equilibrium between the goal of intentional living and the quest for economic viability. For homesteaders, income generation becomes a weapon for empowerment, enabling them to exercise greater control over their financial destinies and minimize their dependence on external systems.

On the other hand, revenue generation has its challenges when living off the grid. The unpredictable nature of income, particularly in conventional agricultural operations, necessitates careful planning and the flexibility to react to changing circumstances. It is necessary to implement measures for diversification and risk management to protect homesteads' financial stability, which unpredictable weather patterns, fluctuations in the market, and seasonal demands can negatively impact. In addition, the use of technology for remote work may provide difficulties regarding dependable internet connectivity, communication infrastructure, and the steep learning curve associated with online platforms.

In addition, the search for chances to generate income may conflict with ethical issues as off-grid homesteaders attempt to strike a balance between the economic feasibility of their endeavors and the environmental sustainability of their practices. Although some activities can generate revenue that may be in perfect agreement with the principles of intentional living, there are also activities that may conflict with ecological harmony. Off-grid homesteaders are responsible for carefully evaluating the environmental impact of the choices they make regarding revenue creation. They must ensure that their participation in economic activities upholds their dedication to living a sustainable and deliberate lifestyle.

The benefits of generating revenue in off-grid life extend beyond financial considerations and can affect the growth of homesteads and the community as a whole. Homesteaders can invest in technology that improves their ability to live self-sufficiently by utilizing sustainable income streams. These technologies include water conservation infrastructure, renewable energy systems, and other technologies. As a result of homesteaders' contributions to local economies, participation in marketplaces, and engagement in trade connections with surrounding communities that are mutually beneficial, income generation becomes a vehicle for community development.

In addition, revenue generation helps off-grid homesteaders develop a sense of autonomy and enhances their sense of empowerment. This offers individuals the means to sustain their homesteading dreams without surrendering their economic independence. The capacity to create revenue while living in remote or rural settings is a significant advantage. Homesteaders can match their financial operations with their values and objectives, whether supporting local markets, promoting sustainability, or contributing to community efforts. This autonomy extends to decision-making procedures, which make it possible for homesteaders to make decisions at their discretion.

Revenue generation in off-grid life is a multifaceted path combining traditional traditions, technology breakthroughs, and conscious choices. In conclusion, this journey is a journey that involves these elements. Off-grid homesteaders are guided in their search for possibilities to generate money congruent with their core beliefs of financial independence, resilience, and sustainability. The transforming impact of revenue generation extends beyond economic considerations to affect the fundamental essence of intentional living. This is true even though there are challenges involved. Income generation becomes a method for individuals to build a lifestyle that is both economically feasible and profoundly aligned with the concepts of self-sufficiency, resilience, and purposeful living. This is because income creation is a means by which individuals may craft an economically viable lifestyle that is deeply aligned with these principles.

Barter and Trade

With off-grid life, chapter, and trade—ancient customs with a long history—find fresh significance and utility. Traditional cashless systems of exchanging products and services provide a flexible and valuable way to address various requirements as people strive for self- sufficiency, sustainability, and intentional living. Barter and trade play a vital role in the complex web of deliberate living, where the rhythms of nature, community, and self-sufficiency converge. They help build relationships, promote resilience, and balance economic independence and intentional living.

Fundamentally, barter is the direct, money-free exchange of commodities or services between people. This age-old custom has been an essential part of human connection throughout all nations and civilizations and predates the invention of money. Barter becomes more critical in the off-grid community as people try to reduce their need for outside economic systems and increase their self-sufficiency. Homesteaders can sell excess produce, handcrafted crafts, and niche talents to meet their varied needs and actively engage in a community-based economic model.

In the context of off-grid living, trade—a more expansive notion that includes the exchange of commodities and services for mutual benefit—complements barter. Trade enables more intricate and varied transactions than swaps, facilitating economic interactions inside and outside the surrounding community. Barter typically indicates a direct exchange. In addition to trading necessities, off-grid homesteaders build relationships beyond the confines of money exchanges, strengthen local economies, and enhance community resilience through trade.

Off-grid living has several advantages for barter and commerce that go well beyond the financial sphere. One main benefit is the capacity to obtain resources and satisfy demands without depending on conventional currency. Barter and trade foster a mutual aid network among homesteaders in a community where each person has unique talents, knowledge, or excess inventory. People can swap what they have for what they need. The concepts of intentional living harmoniously align with the sense of community, shared responsibility, and cooperation that this economic interdependence promotes.

Additionally, trade and barter support the growth of a robust and independent local economy. Off-grid homesteaders can lessen their reliance on foreign markets and protect themselves from the ups and downs of the world economy by conducting business locally. Individuals actively contribute to building a more independent and cohesive community, which aligns with the values of sustainability, resilience, and intentional living.

For off-grid homesteaders, bartering and trading also promote a sense of empowerment and independence. The capacity to exchange goods and services directly allows people to take charge of their financial futures in a world where intricate financial institutions and international markets frequently rule the day. Homesteaders can intentionally choose the sources of their goods, the character of their economic exchanges, and the principles that guide their business dealings thanks to barter and trade.

But living off the grid and engaging in barter and commerce comes with challenges. The absence of a common currency might make it more difficult to assess the worth of goods or services, which can result in negotiations that call for clear communication and community consensus. Furthermore, specific products or services might need to be more readily available, which makes it challenging to find compatible parties for a reasonable trade. Homesteaders need to overcome these obstacles by being open with one another, adaptable, and prepared to change as the dynamics of a swap and trading system do.

Despite these difficulties, the transformative power of barter and exchange in off-grid living is demonstrated by its intentionality, community building, and resilience choices. People who barter and trade cultivate a flexible and adaptive mindset in the face of economic uncertainty, actively attending to the needs and goals of the community. The interconnection of commodities, services, and skills within the community fosters a sense of shared purpose and general well-being, which creates a web of relationships that transcends simple economic transactions.

Furthermore, because barter and trade reduce the environmental impact of conventional consumption, they align with sustainable living ideas. People can lessen the carbon footprint caused by large-scale production and transportation by trading goods and services locally. This environmentally conscious approach stresses responsible resource management and helps to cultivate a lifestyle that is in harmony with the environment.

Traditional knowledge and skills are also vitally preserved and transmitted through barter and trade. People who trade goods and services help to protect farming methods, artisanal crafts, and other abilities that might be necessary for off-grid living. This information sharing ensures that essential skills are passed down through the generations within the community and promotes a sense of cultural continuity.

Trade and barter also help build a strong and cohesive community network. Mutual reliance on each other for essential goods and services fosters mutual support and confidence. Community members may rely on one another for support when things are tough, establishing a safety net beyond the confines of conventional economic structures. In the context of off-grid living, this collective resilience is critical when self-sufficiency and mutual assistance are fundamental to the way of life.

To summarize, barter and trade are essential to off-grid living that connects purposeful decisions, communal resilience, and economic freedom. The age-old customs of direct trade and mutual gain are becoming more and more relevant as people try to reduce their dependency on outside economic systems and promote independence. Notwithstanding obstacles, barter and trade have a profoundly transformational effect that goes beyond economic factors to influence the fabric of purposeful living. Barter and trade become more than just financial exchanges in the dynamic dance between economic independence and community interdependence; they become strands that weave together a resilient, sustainable, and purposeful way of life in off-grid communities.

CONCLUSION

Ultimately, "The Independent Homesteader: A Handbook for Off-Grid Living Success" becomes a thorough manual that integrates sustainability, purposeful living, and self-sufficiency. This guidebook illuminates the complex dance of deliberate choices, giving readers a road map for overcoming obstacles and appreciating the benefits of living off the grid. Every chapter provides a building brick for creating a lifestyle that is in tune with the cycles of nature, from the fundamentals of mental readiness to the valuable elements of sustainable building techniques.

The first step in the trip is realizing that living off the grid is a solid commitment to resilience, autonomy, and environmental stewardship rather than just a lifestyle choice. Every chapter opens up like a gold mine of information, giving readers a comprehensive grasp of the variables impacting place selection, climate considerations, legal and regulatory issues, and the revolutionary effects of incorporating technology into homesteading.

The manual becomes a valuable resource for individuals who aspire to construct a house and establish a sanctuary with a strong foundation in sustainable practices as the story moves through the fundamentals of construction, sustainable building techniques, and alternative power sources. Investigating rainwater collection, well systems, water conservation, and organic farming methods reveals the keys to coexisting peacefully with the land and developing a way of life that benefits people and the environment.

The comprehensive vision of the independent homesteader is highlighted in the chapters on food preservation methods, livestock integration, and permaculture concepts. The complexity of skill development, communication strategies, and internet resources are explained to the reader, highlighting the significance of flexibility and connectedness in the quest for self-sufficiency.

The manual explores the age-old customs of barter and trade in its last chapters, providing an insight into the economic interdependence that creates thriving off-grid communities. The journey's ending serves as more than just a summary of facts; it's an invitation to a life-changing adventure toward successful off-grid living—a way of life where deliberate decisions, sustainability, and resilience come together to weave a fabric of freedom and contentment.

Thank you for buying and reading/ listening to our book. If you found this book useful/ helpful please take a few minutes and leave a review on the platform where you purchased our book. Your feedback matters greatly to us.